Successful Reading Assessments and Interventions for Struggling Readers

Previously Published Works

Teaching and Learning in the (dis)Comfort Zone: A Guide for New Teachers and Literacy Coaches (Palgrave 2010)
   By Deborah Ann Jensen, Jennifer A. Tuten, Yang Hu, and Deborah B. Eldridge

Successful Reading Assessments and Interventions for Struggling Readers

Lessons from Literacy Space

Deborah Ann Jensen and
Jennifer A. Tuten

palgrave
macmillan

SUCCESSFUL READING ASSESSMENTS AND INTERVENTIONS FOR STRUGGLING READERS
Copyright © Deborah Ann Jensen and Jennifer A. Tuten, 2012.

First published in 2012 by
PALGRAVE MACMILLAN®
in the United States—a division of St. Martin's Press LLC,
175 Fifth Avenue, New York, NY 10010.

Where this book is distributed in the UK, Europe and the rest of the world,
this is by Palgrave Macmillan, a division of Macmillan Publishers Limited,
registered in England, company number 785998, of Houndmills,
Basingstoke, Hampshire RG21 6XS.

Palgrave Macmillan is the global academic imprint of the above companies
and has companies and representatives throughout the world.

Palgrave® and Macmillan® are registered trademarks in the United States,
the United Kingdom, Europe and other countries.

ISBN: 978–1–137–02863–1 (hc)
ISBN: 978–1–137–02864–8 (pbk)

Library of Congress Cataloging-in-Publication Data

Jensen, Deborah Ann.
    Successful reading assessments and interventions for struggling
readers : lessons from literacy space / Deborah Ann Jensen,
Jennifer A. Tuten.
        p. cm.
        ISBN 978–1–137–02863–1 (hardback)—
        ISBN 978–1–137–02864–8 ()
        1. Reading—Remedial teaching. 2. Reading—Ability testing.
    I. Tuten, Jennifer A. II. Title.

LB1050.5.J46 2012
372.43—dc23   2012021440

A catalogue record of the book is available from the British Library.

Design by Newgen Imaging Systems (P) Ltd., Chennai, India.

First edition: December 2012

10 9 8 7 6 5 4 3 2 1

My dad was never without a book next to his armchair or beside his bed. Fiction and nonfiction, suspense, adventure, to entertain and to learn; he knew the value of books and perhaps he would have valued this one was well. So this one is for him, my dad, Walter William Jensen, with love.

Deborah Ann Jensen

In an old childhood Polaroid, my dad and I lounge in a hammock, reading a picture book. It reminds me of my dad's love of his children and of literacy. Howard Lincoln Levine was a wonderful writer, voracious reader, and always supportive parent.

Jennifer A. Tuten

Contents

Illustrations

Figures

Tables

Appendices

Preface

Reading at Literacy Space Is Like Reading a Book at My Grandma's—Alex, Age 8

When Alex started attending Literacy Space, a one-year, after-school, tutoring program, he was a struggling reader, turned off by books and reading. He turned his back on books and anything that seemed to resemble life in a classroom. But through his work with one of our graduate students, he learned, he too was a reader and found the joy books had to offer even in an academic setting. When he told Lindsay, his tutor, that he found reading at Literacy Space as comfortable as when he reads with his grandma, we knew our work with Alex had been successful.

Our Program

Literacy Space was created almost ten years ago as a two-semester practicum component in our Master's in Literacy Education program. In our program, graduate students are required to complete two semesters of a supervised practicum, offered back-to-back semesters for three credits each, during which they work continuously with the same child. The children who come to Literacy Space are young elementary school children attending public, charter, or private schools in New York City. They represent a variety of cultures, religions, ethnic, and socioeconomic backgrounds; may be living with a single parent, two parents, or in a multigenerational or multifamily structure; come from homes where attitudes about schools and learning may be different from our own; and many have a first language other than English.

During the two semesters, our graduate students had an opportunity to gain in-depth knowledge of their tutee's literacy development and interests and then to respond with carefully crafted interventions. Since the experience for both graduate students and children extends for two semesters, graduate students have the opportunity to reflect on their practice, integrate their learning, and individually tailor activities, materials, and sessions to the needs of the children with whom they work. We meet in an open room filled with a variety to trade books, art materials, games, manipulatives, computers, books on tape, puppets, and more allowing instruction to be individualized and also recognize the social dimension of literacy learning. Part of each session is allocated to a small group so that tutors and children work, read, and play together.

About This Book

This book has grown out of our experiences working with and learning from our graduate students (almost all certified, working, urban teachers) and a diverse group of struggling readers. It is a book about our own reflection on the process of developing a program of assessment and intervention by watching, listening, and learning about the various roadblocks children face on their road to literacy. It is a book about what our graduate students have accomplished, the tools they have found to be helpful, the materials they used, the books they employed, and the relationships they established with each other and the families of the children who attend Literacy Space.

Over the past ten years, we have found several patterns in the roadblocks children have experienced in literacy learning as they arrive at Literacy Space. We share what we have learned, not as a prescription, but as a starting point or suggestion about the children we have met. We refer to our graduate students as teachers to differentiate our students from the children with whom our teachers work. The names of the teachers and children are pseudonyms. The profiles we offer are a composite of the children with whom we have worked at Literacy Space. As we share our stories and experiences, we will often use the singular I instead of we in order to stay true to the lived experiences.

About the Organization of This Book

The opening chapter, "Literacy Space," discusses the development and considerations of our two-semester practicum. Sharing what we have learned from our research, from our observations, and from our experiences, the reader will understand our overall framework and the orientation we use in working with our teachers and struggling readers. It is in this chapter that we discuss how each child who comes to Literacy Space is given individualized attention, not a prescribed program of evaluation and instruction.

Chapter 2, "Innovations of Literacy Space," pays attention to the details, which make our program different than other after school tutoring programs. We discuss the materials, opportunities, how our overall framework for the two-semester course is actualized in the work being done in Literacy Space. It is in this chapter that we share the starting point of developing an individual profile on each of the children who arrives at Literacy Space.

Each of chapters 3 through 8 discuss a different type of struggling reader we have met in Literacy Space. Although we warn against pigeon holing any child, we have found some common patterns within our struggling reader population. Each of these chapters in organized in the same manner: an overview of the child, research presentation on the type of interference in literacy acquisition including instructional suggestions, background tools to discover more about the child, assessment tools, both informal and formal, used to uncover areas of struggle, plans for intervention and instruction used with the child, and reflection.

Chapter 3 focuses on the child who comes from a monolingual, non-English-speaking or bilingual home. Chapter 4 focuses on the children who just need some more time to acquire the literacy they need to perform to the teacher's expectation. Chapter 5 talks about disengaged children, some of who have had fragmented instruction. Chapter 6 discusses the children who are great decoders but have yet to discover the message of print. Chapter 7 focuses on the child who might have a learning disability that interferes with literacy acquisition, and chapter 8 discusses the older child who brings not only literacy complications but also feelings of inadequacy to the tutoring session.

Chapter 9, "Bringing It to Your Classroom," shares what our teachers have taken from their experiences in Literacy Space and used in their classrooms. We discuss how teachers may implement this experience into their own school setting.

Chapter 10, "Involving Parents, Caregivers, and Families," shares the different workshops, family nights, relationships, and conversations we have found helpful to our program. We believe it is necessary to reach out and involve families and we discuss the importance of and ways to create those relationships.

We believe that our stories, experiences, and suggestions will ring true for many readers. When Lindsay shared what Alex had told her, there were tears of joy in her eyes and in our eyes, too. What we have tried to do in our work with teachers and struggling readers could not have been more evident in Alex's claim to have found the joy of reading.

Acknowledgments

Once a week, over two semesters, parents, caregivers, and babysitters travel by subway, bus, or car to bring a struggling reader to Literacy Space, often with a sibling or two in tow. They come from public, charter, and private schools all over New York City. At the same time, across New York City and its suburbs, our teachers are closing up their classrooms and rushing to the college in time to greet the children and their families. We watch through the year as both children and teachers grow and learn from each other, as they challenge us to grow along with them. We are touched by their dedication. This book is for all of our teachers, children, and families of Literacy Space.

1
Literacy Space

Every child deserves excellent reading teachers because teachers make a difference in children's reading achievement and motivation to read... Excellent reading teachers also motivate children, encourage independent learning, have high expectations for achievement, and help children who are having difficulty. They understand that reading development begins well before children enter school and continues throughout the school years—and beyond.

—International Reading Association (*Position Statement on Reading Teachers*)

Recent research demonstrates that skilled, knowledgeable teachers are the most important factor in supporting children to become strong readers and writers (Allington, 2006). Our work as teacher educators, with teachers, children, and families in our Master's in Literacy Education program is informed by our commitment to prepare excellent teachers to teach the culturally, economically, and linguistically diverse children in our communities so that they attain academic excellence. It is our goal to embrace the teachers enrolled in our literacy program, further develop the knowledge they bring to Literacy Space (the clinical component of their program) and push them to be creative, reflective, and adaptive literacy leaders while also increasing their instructional abilities and knowledge base. After completing our Master's in Literacy Education program, we intend to send to the workplace reading specialists "who can provide instruction, assessment, and leadership for the reading program" (International Reading Association, 2000, n.p.). In this chapter, we discuss the genesis and rationale for Literacy Space, goals for our teachers, children, and families, and finally, an overview of the book's organization.

Context for Change

Several years ago, we had the unique opportunity and challenge to implement changes in our college's Master's in Literacy Education program, specifically the practicum or clinical component toward the end of the program. While we were required to conform to our state's certification requirements for content and fieldwork hours, we were free to devise experiences for teachers that would enable them to translate their prior theoretical understandings of literacy development into effective practice. We also acknowledged the increasing pressures and tension our teachers were facing as schools wrestled with the mandates of No Child Left Behind Act of 2001. Our goal was to create a practicum experience in which teachers could use data from informal and formal assessments to develop instruction in a manner that would allow them to integrate and adapt a wide range of instructional strategies into data-driven lessons. We were clear that to be effective literacy teachers and coaches, our students, who we call "teachers" in this book, needed to construct and implement strong intervention plans rather than to rely on commercially prepared remedial programs while working with a struggling reader.

From our extensive work with novice teachers (Jensen et al., 2010), we understood that teachers need assistance in navigating the accountability demands and the curriculum mandated at their schools in order to teach struggling readers effectively without losing their curricula and instructional decision-making freedoms. Although their initial teacher preparation programs had exposed them to theoretical and conceptual frameworks for effective reading instruction, nonetheless, they needed time, support, and opportunities to put that knowledge into practice. In the current educational landscape where test scores may be used as the sole determinant of effective teaching and student learning, teachers experience enormous pressures. As a result, teachers walk a tight rope between developing formative assessments and delivering targeted instruction responsive to individual children's needs and focus on preparation for high-stakes mandated curriculum and tests. When test scores drive the curriculum, children's literacy capabilities are often lost and children's individual reading differences are ignored (Wilson et al., 2005). "While policy makers may embrace the idea of high stakes testing to 'control' the educational system, this testing invariably results in the narrowing of curriculum and a distinct reduction in the variety of instructional methods" (Cobb and White, 2006, p. 32). The key for teachers, especially those participating in Literacy Space, is to focus on documenting the literacy development of students and carefully analyzing data to inform instruction (Cobb, 2003; Johnston, 2003; Mokhtari, et al., 2007).

One of our biggest challenges as teacher educators is to prepare our teachers to work with struggling readers, not just in a tutoring structure such as Literacy Space but in their own classrooms and schools as reading specialists and coaches. For data to effectively inform instruction, teachers must make distinctions among the results they collect from a variety of assessment tools and high-stakes tests. We believed teachers should implement a multidimensional approach to assessment and instruction, value information from multiple sources, and develop and implement an informed instructional plan based on the child's literacy strengths and vulnerabilities. We expect them to value the information each tool yields and to develop the ability to integrate the findings into a carefully constructed profile of the children's literacy strengths and limitations. "In order to apply what might be modeled by university professors, students must have the opportunity to assist the performance of young learners in an authentic practicum context so that instructors have ongoing opportunities to influence student learning as it unfolds" (Colby and Atkinston, 2004 p. 360). We examined our own theoretical understandings, our beliefs about teaching and learning, in order to design an experience for our teachers, the children, and their families in Literacy Space.

Rationale for Literacy Space

Traditionally, the reading specialist was charged with assessing struggling readers using standardized assessments, and delivering an intervention that targeted isolated reading deficiencies in a pull-out program, in one-on-one or small group instruction in a separate, isolated space (Carr, 2003). The traditional program, often referred to as a skill-deficit model, did not seek to find students' strengths, only their weaknesses. The teacher was called a Remedial Reading Teacher, reflecting the instructional stance of this model. The original literacy specialist program and classroom space we inherited was a large conference area and a collection of small "tutoring" rooms nearby reflecting a more traditional program that was in place before the redesign of our master's program.

During the 1980s and 1990s, a major shift in understanding of the literacy acquisition process emphasized the importance of authentic reading and writing for all learners including those struggling with literacy (Balajthy and Lipa-Wade, 2003). Instead of looking at reading, writing, speaking, listening, and viewing, as separate and distinct skills to be mastered one at a time, these domains were understood as interrelated and interdependent. Assessment, in this new framework, shifted from the deficit model and recognized the role of students' strengths as well as their limitations in their literacy development. The unique experiences that the child brings to the tutoring situation, his or her strengths and vulnerabilities, can provide the teacher with important information about his or her literacy acquisition and stage of literacy development. The responsive teacher, now a literacy specialist or coach, needs to be attuned to the differences among the learners in her classroom (Cobb, 2004).

Today, many of our teachers are handed a scripted program determined by their school or district. Teachers are faced with dilemmas when the script fails to be effective with their students. They begin to doubt what they have come to know about student engagement, their knowledge and beliefs about good literacy instruction, and often do not have the expertise to know how to keep the script and imposed methodologies at arms reach while integrating what they know is best of their students. "Thus, the culprit may not be scripts and programs per se, but the mandate that teachers follow them submissively, unreflectively, and unresponsively, whether or not readers benefit" (Margolis and McCabe, 2006, p. 435).

The diverse learning styles, backgrounds, cultures, and other unique characteristics students bring to classrooms, would be ignored if teachers were mandated to follow scripts without recognizing these differences. Johnson-Parsons (2010) reminded us how important differences can be.

In schools, there are differences about goals and about teaching; differences of background—economic, ethnic, gender; differences of philosophy—political, educational, personal; differences of interest and specialization of grade level or discipline; and so on. All such differences are opportunities for learning, if they are allowed expression and respect. (p. 289).

Roller (1996) demonstrated how important it was for children's learning to be respected and recognized. The children "need teachers who are committed to reaching out to parents, adapting their instruction, partnering with colleagues, and using innovative instructional approaches to decrease failure of struggling readers" (Johnson, 2009, p. 161).

Similarly, Jenkins (2009) asserted, "Struggling readers need teachers who are committed to reaching out to parents, adapting their instruction, partnering with colleagues, and using innovative instructional approaches to decrease failure for struggling readers," (p. 161).

Teachers require more than instructional manuals and scripts, the latest materials; they benefit from a practicum experience, which offers them an opportunity to implement their pedagogical and theoretical knowledge in an arena where they receive targeted feedback and participate in focused discussion. According to Putnam and Borko (2000), it is important for novices to work alongside experienced teachers. They claim positive effects combining university-based course work with field experiences, in our case Literacy Space, where authentic and educational activities are similar to what practitioners actually do in the schools.

Our goal, then, was to put into place a program for our teachers consistent with our beliefs about assessment and intervention, teacher preparation, family involvement, and to use the physical space in a way that advertised that we were a community of learners who had found the joy of reading.

Discussion of Literacy Program and How These Courses Fit In

Our Masters' in Literacy Education program leads to a state professional certification in Literacy Education birth through grade 6. We have recently added an additional program leading to certification in grades 7–12. Most of our graduates continue to teach in classrooms. Some have become literacy coaches, grade level leaders, mentor teachers, reading specialists, resource room teachers, and curriculum specialists. The program is designed to provide courses in content knowledge of reading and writing, pedagogical skills of literacy instruction, problem-solving skills required to assess learning difficulties and construction and implementation of differentiated instruction, as well as leadership skills in literacy education. Evidence-based practice and fieldwork are integrated in every course to provide our teachers opportunities to integrate graduate study with the realities and challenges of teaching literacy diverse classroom settings.

Drawing on the work of Hermann and Sarracino (1993), Roskos, et al. (2000), and Tatem (2004), we designed a two-course sequence in our clinical experience for our graduate students to meet the multifaceted demands of literacy specialists in diverse schools. We wanted to provide teachers time to translate research-based strategies into classroom practices (NICHD, 2000), to work collaboratively in order to narrow the research-to-practice gap (Greenwood and Maheady, 2001), and to take cues from the children they were teaching (Pearson, 2003). We called the two-course sequence Literacy Space. That title, for us, represented the newly designed physical room that we created for the tutoring program, as well the idea of flexibility or space for children, tutors, and families in which to explore and develop literacy abilities. The two courses are usually taken in the last two semesters of our teachers' master's program. Some of the prerequisite courses include Language and Literacy in Early Childhood Education, Instructional Approaches to Literacy, and Literacy Assessment before enrolling in these cap stone courses. It is here that teachers are given time and space to translate their knowledge of literacy instruction gained in their coursework and professional experience into their focused tutoring of children struggling with literacy acquisition.

Teachers now take what they have learned about literacy assessment, and have the opportunity to apply them in an instructional setting with the support of both instructors and colleagues. As instructors, we worked with our teachers in order for them to value the information each assessment tool yields and to develop the ability to integrate the findings into a carefully constructed profile of the child's literacy strengths and limitations. This provided the foundation for the development and implementation of an informed and individualized intervention plan.

Organization for Assessment and Instruction

Time, for both teachers and children, in Literacy Space is limited. The once a week for two-semester format requires the teachers to utilize a carefully planned instructional framework that is closely aligned to assessment findings and monitored closely to identify how intervention has been successful. Many of our teachers have not had the opportunity to use a range of assessment tools nor to determine how to utilize these assessments in planning for instruction in their own classrooms. Through our ongoing supervision of teachers in Literacy Space, teachers are supported in learning how to scaffold instruction, modify, and attempt to improve instruction based on the ongoing observations and assessments of needs and progress. Our teachers use a form at the end of each session to help them reflect on the day's instruction, observational data, assessment data, and help to plan for the next lesson. A completed form below (figure 1.1) illustrates the

---

DAILY RECORD OF ACTIVITIES

Student: _____Mack_____ Meeting Number 1 (second semester)_____
Date: _____2/1_____ Tutor: _____Carl_____

Activity: What did you do?	Diagnostic Implication: What did you learn about the student's strengths and/or vulnerabilities while participating in this activity?	Reflection: What does this mean for further assessment and/or intervention plans?
Riddles "What Am I?"	• Had trouble identifying the objects but not reading the riddles • Loved doing them	• Build on comprehension • Work on slowing down wile reading • Consider oral reading
Catch up/see what he is reading	• Reading short stories • Gave up on chapter book	• Find a chapter book to read with him • Look at interest inventory for topic of interest
Writing about one thing we did over break	• Not motivated • Needed prompts • No details in writing or illustration	• Consider lessons on revision • Study illustrations in books to show relationship between writing and pictures
Community Share Readers' Theatre: Three Little Pigs	• Held back from choosing part • Read part quickly and without expression	• Consider reading rate and what it means to comprehension

Plan for Next Session:

1. Focus on word attach strategies/context clues
2. Use riddles as session opener—discuss inferencing in riddles

Additional Comments:

Before I build comprehension I want to focus on word attack strategies that will force him to focus on what is going on in the stories—take a break from works and look at pictures

---

Figure 1.1   Completed Daily Record of Activities

type of information that the teachers record after a day's session. The form called the Daily Record of Activities can be found in the back of this chapter.

The course meets for two and a half hours each week. The first part of the class meeting is devoted to time with the children beginning with one-on-one sessions and ending with community time where small groups of teachers and children meet to play games, read together, or respond to what they have read using crafts, drama, or readers' theatre formats. It is during this time that teachers have the opportunity to observe their struggling reader participating in authentic literacy situations. Teachers also have the opportunity to participate in

The last hour of the class is devoted to discussion of what was learned about the children, what questions arose from what was learned, and what direction would be the logical next step in terms of further assessment and intervention.

Goals for Our Teachers

In redesigning the clinical part of our program, we articulated a clear set of goals for teachers. What would a graduate of our literacy program acquire during their program that they may not develop elsewhere? It was imperative for our teachers to develop expertise in literacy development and instruction, not just for struggling readers but to take what they learned from working with a child in Literacy Space to their classrooms. We also believed it was critical to provide the experience of being part of a professional community in order to understand the benefits of professional collaboration and the opportunity it offers for continued professional growth beyond graduate school. Finally, we knew that in order to effectively teach the children in their classes our teachers needed to acquire the ability to work with diverse children and their families.

Expertise in Literacy Development, Assessment, and Instruction

Parsons and colleagues (2011) found that when teachers are given both the freedom and the guidance to use high-level literacy instruction, they design lessons in line with effective literacy instruction and see positive outcomes in their students. Similarly, Guthrie (2004) found that when a teacher views engaged reading as a worthy practice in and of itself, she would use more authentic literature, well-formed textbooks in content domains, and materials with academically sub-stantive content. She will say to herself, "Books are an important part of life and I want you to use them well" (p. 1).

For our teachers mandated to use scripted programs or who are given little curricular responsibility, our goal is for them to unpack commercial scripts and find ways to integrate methods to gain con-trol and to help eliminate the negative effects of programs that ignore readers differences and needs in their own classrooms (Margolis and McCabe, 2006). By requiring teachers to create instruction based on the needs of their struggling readers in Literacy Space, teachers are challenged to use knowledge of literacy development and best prac-tices in order to meet the needs of the child rather than keep pace with a program. We work with our teachers in learning how assessment and learners' interests can be used to inform instruction.

The results of standardized tests and adequate yearly progress often determine the extent of federal and state involvement; many teachers are experiencing the tension between implementing assessments and methods of instruction responsive to individual children's needs and those they are mandated to use in the form of commercial instructional packages. Invernizzi et al. (2005) explored the importance of selecting assessment tools that are grounded in scientific research and provide teachers with instructionally useful information. In fact, there are negative consequences for students when there is a mismatch between assessment tools and instruction (Taylor and Nolan, 2005). Bean and her colleagues (2002) found that the majority of reading specialists they surveyed used most often informal means of assessment, such as observations, running records, and products produced by children.

Although children working with a reading specialist experienced differences in curriculum from specialist to specialist, McGill-Franzen and Allington (2005) reported that the curriculum "was every bit as routinized as their work in the general classroom, with no evidence that instruction was personalized to address the needs or performance of individuals" (p. 177). One-size-fits-all programs for assessment and instruction are adverse to effective practice (Lipson and Wixson, 1997).

Ability to Make Data Informed Decisions about Struggling Readers and Writers

We believe that active engagement in meaningful literacy activities is the key to proficiency for our struggling readers. Similarly, we believe that teachers will become most effective through intense engage-ment in real teaching experiences. The decisions we made about the program stemmed from the theoretical rationale that students who are given choices also feel ownership of their learning. With owner-ship, students dig deeper for meaning, are more likely to monitor for understanding, and, given choices, will express their knowledge in a variety of ways (Guthrie, 2004). Students are given opportunities to respond to literature through many hands-on activities. Puppets, flannel pieces, craft items, creations of recipes, are just a few of the methods children responded to the books they read in Literacy Space (a more thorough description is given in chapter 2). Literacy Space has an extensive library of poetry, nonfiction, fiction, and magazines to be matched to children's interests and curiosities.

Schön (1987) discussed the practicum as a setting for learning a practice. "The practicum is a virtual world, relatively free of the pres-sures, distractions, and risks of the real world, to which, nevertheless, it refers" (p. 37). Morris (2011) asserts that a practicum experience can change a teacher's attitude toward struggling readers. "Don't underestimate the power of this clinical teaching experience. Seeing a struggling reader begin to succeed—and knowing that one's teach-ing led to this success—can be a career-changing experience. From that point on, the teacher may view differently his or her ability (and responsibility) to help children who struggle with reading" (p. 56).

Understand the Power of a Professional Learning Community

Steiner (2000) asserts that when adults work in collaboration, they create zones of proximal development for each other. He goes on to claim that collaboration can be a mirror for each other provid-ing a change to understand one's habits, styles, working methods, and beliefs through comparison and contract with other collabora-tors. When a diverse group of teachers have the opportunity to come together as a community of learners, they draw on and incorporate each other's expertise into their own instructional situations (Putnam and Borko, 2000).

When Roskos et al. (2000) studies the teacher's role in creating a system to support student learning in a reading clinic, they incorpo-rated time when teachers would reflect on the one-to-one tutoring sessions with their colleagues. Not only could concepts be examined and text-based knowledge interwoven into conversations, but colleagues could seek advice from colleagues. They discovered:

Although learning by doing also seems critical, what may need greater emphasis is not the actual "doing" or practice teaching, but the learning it affords made visible through artifacts, such as detailed field notes, checklists, or written self-reflections, and well assisted regular debriefings about specific teaching incidents (Roskos et al., p. 232).

Coming together as a professional community allows its participants to reflect on their own practices, knowledge, and theories. Fredricksen (2010) claims that we need to "go public" with what we come to know about our practice. "When we go public with what we think we have learned, it allows us to put that knowledge into conversation with other, which in turn, creates opportunities for refining and expanding our knowledge" (Fredricksen, 2010, p. 24).

Based on our belief that learning is collaborative and needs to "go public," the teachers and instructor meet for an hour after the children leave Literacy Space. During this time, we gather to wrestle with implementing text-based knowledge, interpreting assessments to determine what it is we have discovered and yet want to know about the children, and the design and putting into practice instructional plans. It is here that real opportunities for learning, decisions about instruction, and time to interact with others to reflect and build knowledge and beliefs related to literacy occur (Mallette et al., 2000).

Development of Understanding and Ability to Engage and Work with Diverse Families

In addition to learning about the children, we also devote time to learning about their families. We embrace a culturally responsive perspective (Gay, 2000) that promotes developing understanding and mutual appreciation of cultural heritage as well as building "bridges of meaningfulness between home and school experiences as well as between academic abstractions and lived sociocultural realities" (p. 29). We learned from the powerful work of Lazar (2004) and Schmidt and Lazar (2011) that we need to address head on the challenges presented by teachers who often have preconceived ideas about children and families who are different, economically, linguistically, racially, or culturally. One fundamental way to move teachers beyond their perspectives is through facilitating deep, sustainable relationships with families. Our goal, according to Schmidt and Lazar (2011), is to support teachers in becoming generative teachers, "cultural mediators,...teachers who try to know their students well and go out of their way to reach out to families. Generative teachers understand that to give children the best education possible, they must learn from students, families, and communities" (p. 16).

Goals for Children and Families

From the outset, we wanted the children and families to experience Literacy Space in a positive way. We wanted the experience to be mutually beneficial and sustaining. While the primary goal was for the children to leave with an increased ability to read and write and reach the level with their classmates, we knew that for any sustained impact, children needed to leave with the joy of reading and an increased motivation to read. We wanted the children to be more confident in their abilities and be able to identify what they knew about their own reading and reading preferences. We wanted the children to feel that they were part of a wider community of readers. We also wanted to outreach to their families and to increase their knowledge of how to support literacy and recognize the importance of home-literacy events.

According to the Center of Educational Policy (2007), despite the significantly increased instructional time that many low-income students spend in reading instruction (often at the expense of subject areas such as science, art, social studies, music, and even recess), there was little evidence that the students benefited from the reforms instituted by Reading First or No Child Left Behind. This supports our view that it is the type of instruction, often not the quantity of time spent on literacy instruction that has a positive impact on student engagement. Time and time again we are reminded that meaningful engagement in literacy is strongly related to reading comprehension, something that the National Reading Panel (NRP) neglected in their report. "Although the NRP endorsed a balanced approach to reading instruction, its meta-analysis said very little about the importance of literacy engagement" (Cummins, 2007, 569).

Although our main goal is to provide intervention in order for the children to keep pace with their more able classmates, we understand that to do this requires us to know the children very well in order to meet their needs as learners. We know that reading failure is not distributed randomly, but is concentrated among schools serving the disadvantaged, minority populations, and English language learners (Lake et al, 2009).

The beginning of their time in Literacy Space is devoted to learning about them as children, their interests, goals, personal histories, passions, culture, and more. "Meeting the needs of all students in reading is essential, and the quality of instruction for linguistically and culturally diverse students is characteristic of quality instruction for all students" (Walker-Dalhouse et al., 2010, p. 70). Because the children who attend Literacy Space are young, their parents and caregivers wait outside the rooms during the tutoring period. We understood that we had an opportunity to bring families into the literacy-learning process in unique ways, to be discussed in later chapters. Our goal for families is help them understand their role in the literacy-learning process and to enable them to understand the particular struggles and strengths of their children.

Patterns of Literacy Disruption

All struggling readers need to catch up to their classmates for a variety of reasons. Many children come to Literacy Space with limited literacy experience. They may have come from homes where books and literacy activities have not been present or valued. Sometimes the types of literacy experiences children do bring to school are not present or valued in the school. Moll and his colleagues (1992) believe that children have "funds of knowledge" that teachers rarely draw upon for use inside the classroom. (We devote chapter 10 to ways to involve parents.)

Environmental and cultural differences may also account for some of the literacy differences of struggling readers compared to their classmates. Language differences may also compound the difficulties of struggling readers in keeping up with their classmates.

Children mature at different rates and so does their literacy development. Differences in auditory and visual development may keep some children from performing at the same level as their classmates.

We have also found that school programs, often scripted, have not worked for some children and they are often left at the wayside.

Too often struggling readers and writers have been clustered together without recognizing that their strengths and vulnerabilities differ from each other. The advantage of identifying subgroups of struggling readers assists us in implementing appropriate intervention strategies (Catts et al., 2003). For whatever reason children have been referred to Literacy Space, they all need to learn the strategies good readers use. They need to be introduced to the joy of reading.

How This Book Is Organized

Over the past ten years of working with our teachers, struggling readers, and their families, we have seen patterns emerge in the work done in Literacy Space. We have also come to recognize the unique aspects of our program. Our book shares these experiences with the reader.

It is important to understand how Literacy Space came into being and the theoretical framework on which it rests, the goals it embraces, and beliefs we hold dear. The design, redesign, constant tweaking and refining happens as we work with more and more teachers and children and learn more about literacy development ourselves as educators. This chapter was written to the reader on our journey in developing Literacy Space over the past ten years.

Literacy Space has many unique characteristics. We are a community of learners and have designed aspects to the program, which advertise our position. From a vast collection and catalog of print materials, crafts, puppets, puzzles, games, computers, and special events such as Family Game Nights and parent workshops, Literacy Space illustrates our belief that we need to support each other and our learning. This is described in chapter 2.

Chapters 3 through 8 describe the patterns of struggles we have seen in Literacy Space. We do not suggest that there is a formula in an approach to any of these but we do want to share the types of struggling readers we have typically encountered, the research we have found on the various types of struggling readers, the tools for assessment we have found to be most valuable, and the types of intervention plans that have been most successful with the children.

One of our goals is to send teachers into the field with increased knowledge and strategies learned working with a struggling reader that they can use in their classrooms. We surveyed our graduates to find what they carried with them from Literacy Space into their classrooms successfully. In chapter 9, we share some of the research on clinical programs and their impact on classroom performance. We also share our survey results and what our graduate had to say about their experience.

Families are so important to the success of struggling readers. We have welcomed the families by inviting them in to special events throughout the two semesters their child, brother, or sister spends in Literacy Space. We often have siblings follow each other from one semester to the next in Literacy Space, a message from parents about their perception of success and support Literacy Space provides. Chapter 10 shares some of the research on parental involvement and the special features offered in Literacy Space for parents and families. Throughout the book, we had used pseudonyms for the teachers and children. Each is a composite of the teachers and children we have worked with over the years and is not any specific person who attended Literacy Space.

References

Allington, R. L. (2006). *What Really Matters for Struggling Readers: Designing Research-Based Programs.* New York: Pearson.

Balajthy, E. and Lipa-Wade, S. (2003). *Struggling Readers: Assessment and Instruction in Grades K-6.* New York: Guilford Press.

Bean, R. M., Cassidy, J., Grumet, J. V., Shelton, D., and Wallis, S. R. (2002). "What do reading specialists do? Results from a national survey." *The Reading Teacher,* 55(8): 736–744.

Carr, K. C. (2003). "Today's reading clinic: How relevant is the graduate reading practicum?" *The Reading Teacher,* 57(3): 256–268.

Catts, H. W., Hogan, T. P., and Fey, M. C. (2003). "Subgrouping poor readers on the basis of individual differences in reading-related abilities." *Journal of Learning Disabilities,* 36(2): 151–164.

Center for Educational Policy. (2007). *Choices, Changes, and Challenges: Curriculum and Instruction in the NCLB Era.* Retrieved March 30, 2011, from http://cep-dc.org.

Cobb, C. (2004). "Tuning on a dime: Making change in literacy classrooms." *The Reading Teacher,* 58(1): 104–106.

———. (2003). "Effective instruction begins with purposeful assessments." *The Reading Teacher,* 57(4): 386–388.

Cobb, J. and White, A. (2006). "High stakes testing, accountability, and pre-scribed direct systematic phonics instruction: A comparison of struggling readers attending a university reading clinic before and after state mandated testing." *Journal of Reading Education,* 32(6): 31–37.

Colby, S. A. and Atkinston, T. S. (2004). "Assisting performance in teaching and learning." *Teacher Education,* 15(4): 351–362.

Cummins, J. (2007). "Pedagogies for the poor? Realigning reading instruction for low-income students with scientifically based reading instruction." *Educational Researcher,* 36(9): 564–572.

Enriquez, G., Jones, S., and Clarke, L. W. (2010). "Turning around our perceptions and practices, then our readers." *The Reading Teacher,* 64(1): 73–76.

Fredricksen, J. E. (2010). "Building conscious competence: Reading our students, sharing our practice." *The New England Reading Association Journal,* 45(2): 17–25.

Gay, G. (2000). *Culturally Responsive Teaching: Theory, Research, and Practice.* New York: Teachers College Press.

Greenwood, C. R. and Maheady, L. (2001). "Are future teachers aware of the gap between research and practice and what should they know?" *Teacher Education and Special Education,* 24(4): 333–347.

Guthrie, J. T. (2004). "Teaching for literacy engagement." *Journal of Literacy Research,* 36(1): 1–30.

Hermann, B. A. and Sarracino, J. (1993). "Restructuring a preservice literacy methods course: Dilemmas and lessons learned." *Journal of Teacher Education,* 44(2): 96–106.

International Reading Association. (2000). *Teaching All Children to Read: The Roles of the Reading Specialist* (A position statement of the International C Document Reproduction Service No. ED438533). Retrieved September 30, 2008, from http://eric.ed.gov/ERICDocs/data/ericdocs2sql/content _storage_01/0000019b/80/ 16/11/d2.pdf

Invernizzi, M. A., Landrum, T. J., Howell, J. L. and Warley, P. (2005). "Toward the peaceful coexistence of test developers, policymakers, and teachers in an era of accountability." *The Reading Teacher,* 58(8): 619–631.

Jenkins, S. (2009). "How to maintain school reading success: Five recommendations from a struggling male reader." *The Reading Teacher,* 63(2): 159–162.

Jensen, D. A., Tuten, J. A., Hu, Y., and Eldridge, D. B. (2010). *Teaching and Learning in the (dis)Comfort Zone: A Guide for New Teachers and Literacy Coaches.* New York: Palgrave MacMillan.

Johnson-Parsons, M. (2010). "Dreaming of collaboration." *Language Arts,* 87(4): 287–295.

Johnston, P. (2003). "Assessment conversations." *The Reading Teacher,* 57(1): 90–92.

Lake, C., Davis, S., and Madden, N. A. (2009). *Effective Programs for Struggling Readers: A Best-Evidence Synthesis.* Baltimore, MD: Johns Hopkins University, Center for Data-Driven Reform in Education. Retrieved March 7, 2012, from www.bestevidence.org/word/strug_read_jun_02_2010.pdf

Lazar, A. M. (2004). *Learning to Be Literacy Teachers in Urban Schools: Stories of Growth and Change.* Newark, DE: International Reading Association.

Lipson, M. and Wixson, K. (1997). *Assessment and Instruction of Reading and Writing Disability: An Interactive Approach* (2nd ed.). New York: Longman.

Mallette, M. H., Kile, R. S., Smith, M. M., McKinney, M., and Readance, J. E. (2000). "Constructing meaning about literacy difficulties: Preservice teachers beginning to think about pedagogy." *Teaching and Teacher Education,* 16 (5): 593–612.

Margolis, H. and McCabe, P. P. (2006). "Motivating struggling readers in an era of mandated instructional practices." *Reading Psychology,* 27(5): 435–455.

McGill-Franzen, A. and Allington, R. (2005). "The gridlock of low reading achievement: Perspectives on practice and policy." In Z. Fang (Ed.) *Literacy Teaching and Learning: Current Issues and Trends* (pp. 173–183). Upper Saddle River, NJ: Pearson Merrill Prentice Hall.

Mokhtari, K., Rosemary, C. A., and Edwards, P. A. (2007). "Making instructional decisions based on data: What, how, and why." *The Reading Teacher,* 61(4): 354–359.

Moll, L., Amanti, C., Neff, D., and Gonzalez, N. (1992). "Funds of knowledge for teaching: Using a qualitative approach to connect homes and school." *Theory into Practice*, 31(2): 32–141.

Morris, D. (2011). "Practicum training for teachers of struggling readers." *Kappan*, 92(8): 54–57.

National Institute of Child Health and Human Development. (2000). *The Report of the National Reading Panel. Teaching Children to Read: An Evidence-Based Assessment of the Scientific Research Literature on Reading and Its Implications for Reading Instruction* (NIH Publication No. 00–4769). Washington DC: US Government Printing Office.

Parsons, S. A., Metzger, S. A., Askew, J. and Carswell, A. R. (2011). "Teaching against the grain: One title 1 school's journal toward project-based literacy instruction." *Literacy Research & Instruction*, 50(1): 1–14.

Pearson, P. D. (2003). The role of the professional knowledge in reading reform. *Language Arts*, 81(1), 14–15.

Putnam R. and Borko, H. (2000). "What do new views of knowledge and thinking have to say about research on teacher learning?" *Educational Researcher*, 29(1): 4–15.

Roller, C. M. (1996). *Variability Not Disability: Struggling Readers in a Workshop Classroom*. Newark, DE: International Reading Association.

Roskos, K., Boehlen, S., and Walker, B. J. (2000). "Learning the art of instructional conversation: The influence of self-assessment on teachers' instructional discourse in a reading clinic." *The Elementary School Journal*, 100(3): 229–253.

Schmidt, P. R. and Lazar, A. M. (2011). *Practicing What We Teach: How Culturally Responsive Literacy Classrooms Make a Difference*. New York: Teachers College.

Schön, D. (1987). *Educating the Reflective Practitioner*. San Francisco, CA: Jossey-Bass.

Steiner, J. V. (2000). *Creative Collaboration*. New York: Oxford University Press.

Tatem, A.W. (2004). "A road map for reading specialists entering schools without exemplary reading programs: Seven quick lessons." *The Reading Teacher*, 58(1): 28–39.

Taylor, C. S. and Nolen, S. B. (2007). *Classroom Assessment: Supporting Teaching and Learning in Real Classrooms*. Upper Saddle River, NJ: Prentice Hall.

Toll, C. A., Nierstheimer, S. L., Lenski, S. D., and Kolloff, P. B. (2004). "Washing out students clean: Internal conflicts in response to preservice teachers' beliefs and practices." *Journal of Teacher Education*, 55(2): 164–176.

Walker-Dalhouse, D., Risko, V. J., Lathrop, K. and Porter, S. (2010). "Helping diverse struggling readers through reflective teaching and coaching." *The Reading Teacher*, 64(1): 70–72.

Wilson, P., Martens, P., and Arya, P. (2005). "Accountability for reading and readers: What the numbers don't tell." *The Reading Teacher*, 58(4): 622–631.

Appendix I-A   Daily Record of Activities

Student _____ Meeting Number _____
Date _____ Tutor _____

Activity: What did you do?	Diagnostic Implication: What did you learn about the student's strengths and/or vulnerabilities while participating in this activity?	Reflection: What does this mean for further assessment and/or intervention plans?
Community Share		

Plan for Next Session:

_____

_____

_____

_____

_____

_____

_____

_____

_____

_____

_____

Additional Comments:

_____

_____

_____

_____

_____

_____

_____

_____

_____

_____

_____

_____

_____

2

Innovations of Literacy Space

There are many after-school reading programs throughout the country. Many, such as ours, are part of a university-based teacher-education program. In this chapter, we discuss the innovative features of Literacy Space and our model of reading, reading assessment, and effective interventions to support the struggling readers.

Literacy Space

In chapter 1, we discussed the theoretical framework that served as a catalyst in our shift from a deficit model of reading assessment and remediation toward one based on children's strengths and learning needs. Embodying that shift is the efforts placed in redesigning the physical space for the tutoring experience. Instead of going off to small tutoring rooms where a tutor and a child would work together, Literacy Space invited collaboration, small group work, and private time for tutor and child to work independently.

Children attend Literacy Space weekly, from 4:30 p.m. until 5:45 p.m. There are sessions Mondays through Thursdays, paralleling the college schedule. A faculty coordinator handles recruitment and scheduling of the children. The children attend a variety of public, private, and charter schools both in our immediate neighborhood and a bus- or subway-ride away. Over time, we've developed close relationships with principals, teachers, and parent coordinators at several schools and are able to work with them to support their struggling students. Some of the children are referred by their teachers, parents of children in our program, and often by our current or former Masters' in Literacy program students, another close bond. We ask families to complete a brief application and submit it to the coordinator. Presently, the applications are in Spanish and English and are available on our newly created website. We do not specifically pre-screen children for this program. There is no cost for the tutoring.

Literacy Space is located in a large, 17-story office type building, one of the college's four buildings. For many children there is excitement at coming to a college. Families often visit the college books store, grab a snack in the cafeteria, or peek into the library and classrooms. Since ours is a large public college, some families become interested in other programs and opportunities to expand their own education. We keep our family room stocked with materials about college programs and have frequently served advisors for families interested in other programs.

The Literacy Space room is a large open room. There are round tables, with colorful chairs. Two tables are smaller, with smaller chairs, most comfortable for younger children. One wall is filled with books. The collection of books in Literacy Space is purposely large and eclectic. There are copies of current children's series books such as *Junie B. Jones* and *Nate the Great*. Bins hold books by topic, reading level, or author. There are joke books, readers' theatre books, alphabet books, books specifically designed to reinforce vowel sounds, digraphs, blends, or word family. There are books for tutors to use as resources when planning lessons. There are chapter books and picture books as well as a small collection of wordless books. We also have amassed a large collection of quality nonfiction books as well. They are also in bins by reading level or subject area such as ocean life that includes books about sharks, penguins, and the coral reef. There is a bin that holds books on knights and one on pyramids. There is a collection of magazines, a shelf of biographies, atlases, and record books. There are even alphabet books in this section on topics such as the Olympics, the galaxy, ballet, and New York State.

Another wall of Literacy Space contains a wide variety of hands-on materials or manipulatives. There are hand puppets, finger puppets, flannel boards with letters and pictures, books with flannel pieces, magnetic letters and words, chalkboards, and white boards. There are puzzles and beach balls with reader response questions written on the different colored panels. Here, we also provide many different kinds of art materials such as crayons, markers, stamp pads, collage materials, scissors with fancy edges, and colored paper. We have highlighting tape, post-its©, and index cards. Games are an additional focus of the materials in Literacy Space. We have commercial games such as Totally Gross Science©, Guess Who©, and Apples to Apples Junior©. We have also created our own games.

Adjacent to the large room is a wide hallway. We have turned this common space into an area for families. There are chairs for the families. The bulletin boards are filled with information and interactive activities for children and families. Opening to this area are four smaller rooms. One of these rooms houses computers and computer activities, another, tape recorders and books on tape, and a third is additional space for families. These rooms, along with several more, are also used by teachers and students when quiet or privacy is needed for a particular assessment or a special activity.

Letters to Families and Schools

By the end of children's first semester at Literacy Space, teachers develop a diagnostic profile of the child's literacy needs and strengths. This profile encapsulates the descriptive data collected throughout the semester, summary and analysis of the assessments given through the semester (discussed later in the chapter), and literacy goals for the next semesters' work. This assignment prepares teachers to develop a professional report. This information is then shared with the child's teacher and the child's family in the form of a letter.

While it is key for teachers to understand how to write a diagnostic report, it is equally important for them to learn how to share, in writing and in conversation, their evaluation of the children with their families, their peers, and their teachers. Teacher write letters to the families, outlining the kinds of assessments implemented, key findings, and suggestions for ways families can support their children at home. We work with teachers to think carefully about how to translate "teacher" terms such as "lexiles" or "phonemic awareness" into terms families can understand. We also discuss and model appropriate tone and register of the letters. In the second semester, teachers write a second letter to families, reviewing the year's progress and presenting suggestions for the future.

The sample below illustrates the content and tone of the letters.

Dear Mr. and Mrs. Martin,

I have enjoyed getting to know and working with May over the course of the past two semesters. It has been a pleasure tutoring such a motivated and hard working student. I have seen May grow as a reader and a writer, and would like to share with you some of her accomplishments.

In September, Maya enjoyed reading, but wasn't confident in reading aloud. I have noticed quite a change in her confidence. Her reading aloud sounds great. Sometimes I think she would be an incredible actress because of the expression that she uses when she reads.

I know that we have discussed working on May's comprehension skills, and this is another area that I have seen great improvement in. We have been reading factual texts including magazines and newspaper articles, to help her comprehension. These texts have been full of facts and new information. May is now a lot more comfortable with this type text. Her vocabulary has also been improving as a result of reading these more difficult nonfiction texts. She has been able to figure out the meaning of unknown words by using different strategies that we have practiced.

May has also improved on analyzing books and poems. We have read two novels that had strong themes. Through writing and also discussions, she has demonstrated that she can find the deeper meaning in these books. She has also been able to begin to understand complex characters and problems. These are skills that May will use in the higher grades.

Over the past two semesters, I have also been working with May on poetry. She has been having fun with this and even wrote some poems. She has been able to analyze the poems and tell me what they mean to her.

I am really impressed with the progress that May has made since I've begun working with her. There are some things that you can do to help further May's comprehension skills. May would benefit from both reading to you and to her brother. She would also benefit from hearing you read to her, in both English and Spanish. You can have discussions about what you read. You can ask her questions about what is happening in the reading and also about what she thinks about the text.

Another great way to help the whole family be involved in helping May's literacy skills would be to have discussions while watching television. You can ask her questions about the problem, solution, characters, and so on. This will help her be able to answer comprehension questions and that will translate into her comprehension while reading.

May has really been enjoying reading poetry as well as science and social studies magazines. You can encourage her to read these types of texts and also have discussions with her about them.

I am extremely proud of the progress that May has made this year. It has been a pleasure working with her and I am confident that she will continue to grow as a reader and writer.

Sincerely,
Anita Lee

Teachers also need to communicate with other teachers. Teachers tutoring at Literacy Space often discover strengths, interests, and effective strategies working with children over two semesters. It's important for them to communicate their insights from the tutoring context without usurping the classroom teachers' role. The sample below illustrates this balance.

Dear Keyasia's third grade teacher:

Over the past few months, I have had the opportunity to work with your student Keyasia in the Literacy Space at Hunter College. I am currently enrolled in the Literacy program at Hunter College, and will be graduating this month with my Master's Degree in Literacy. This is also my third year as a head teacher at a private preschool in lower Manhattan. Based on my experiences both as a classroom teacher and what I have learned at Hunter, I feel that I have been able to effectively identify as well as address some of Keyasia's specific strengths and vulnerabilities as a reader.

Since I only met Keyasia for the first time in January, our first few sessions were spent getting to know each other. Through oral interview questions, conversations, and writing prompts I learned that Keyasia loves likes to play Nintendo D. S. and that she also plays the violin. She also enjoys reading picture books by Dr. Seuss and taking care of her two pet turtles. Keyasia is an extremely outgoing, animated, and friendly child. She is very easygoing and approaches learning new things with a positive attitude. Keyasia has a positive attitude toward reading, but made it clear that she prefers reading aloud rather than reading silently. She says this is because when she reads in her head she gets distracted easily. Keyasia also informed me that in school she listens to teacher read-alouds, participates in a small reading group, and given the opportunity to read silently every day.

After our first few sessions together, Keyasia and I had established a comfortable relationship, and I began to use various types of formal and informal assessment tools with her. These assessments focused on the areas of oral language, phonological awareness, fluency, comprehension, strategic knowledge, retelling, spelling, and writing. The formal assessment tools I used with Keyasia were running records and story retelling guides. I also made some informal observations about Keyasia during discussions while interacting with another adult and child in the Literacy Space. Other informal assessments included looking at drawings, writing samples, engaging in conversations, listening to Keyasia read aloud, and observing Keyasia while she read silently. After assessing Keyasia's literacy skills and determining her major strengths and vulnerabilities as a reader, I chose a few specific areas to focus on for the remainder of the semester.

Our sessions together followed the same structure each week, which made the expectations clear for Keyasia and allowed us to cover all of the necessary areas of reading and writing. I began each session with giving Keyasia a writing prompt to read and to respond. The purpose of these prompts was to increase her stamina for writing. The prompts were very informal and consisted of questions about her favorite things, what she did on vacation, something she finds scary, and so on. In order to increase the length and content of her response, each week I asked her to provide more details. When we first started in January, Keyasia told me that she did not really enjoy writing, and she seemed to be more confidant giving an oral response to a question. I definitely think this has changed and that Keyasia feels much more comfortable with writing and is happy to share her thoughts and opinions with those around her. The second part of our sessions together was called "word work" and consisted of different activities related to spelling patterns as well as letters and their corresponding sounds. Keyasia's tutor from last semester expressed this as an area of concern, so I wanted to make sure that these needs were addressed. During this time, Keyasia completed several word sorts, which focused recognizing different vowel sounds. In addition to completing the actual sorts, she was asked to add additional words that fit the specific patterns as well as write a sentence or two about why she sorted the words the way she did. We also played a game called "word detective" where Keyasia and I walked around the building to find different words with certain letters or groups of letters. Over the course of the semester, I have noticed that Keyasia has shown a great deal of improvement in spelling and manipulating letters and sounds.

The third part of our sessions included types of reading activities where both of us were involved. At the beginning of the semester, I did a running record with Keyasia that informed me that her independent reading level was a Fountas and Pinnell level L, making her instructional reading level an M. It seemed that the only thing holding her back from reading an independent level M was her comprehension. She was having difficulty retelling stories and over relied on the text for her answers. Based on these assessments and observations, Keyasia and I worked a lot on retelling a story this semester and how it is important to pay attention to the plot and story elements. Together we worked on recalling events from a story without having to read a specific sentence or phrase directly from the text. She achieved this by practicing putting sentences into her own words. Having these skills will enable Keyasia to understand and enjoy a story more thoroughly. During our earlier sessions together, I read aloud to Keyasia while she listened and responded, and during our later sessions, we began to read various texts together alternating page by page. We also worked on several strategies for monitoring comprehension such as summarizing, rereading, and asking questions. One of Keyasia's main strengths as a reader is her ability to read aloud and her ability and confidence have only increased over time. When Keyasia and I first started working together, she was not reading chapter books and had a preference for picture books. Over the past few months, Keyasia has expressed more of an interest in chapter books and is able to read and understand them. Finally, the last part of our sessions provided Keyasia with the opportunity to read silently. Since her tutor from last semester expressed this as an area of concern and that Keyasia made it clear she did not prefer reading silently, I felt that this was a very important area of focus for the semester. I am proud to say that Keyasia has grown tremendously in this area, and is at ease when it comes to reading silently. When we first started in January, she was using headphones while reading silently to help her focus, but by the end of our sessions, she felt that she no longer needed that support.

I think it is important that we continue to encourage Keyasia to practice reading at home and in school in order to build her confidence, increase her stamina for reading, and improve her comprehension and retelling abilities. There are many other things Keyasia can do in the classroom to work on her comprehension and retelling as well. While Keyasia is reading, it might be useful to ask her some comprehension questions and encourage her to give an oral retelling of a story. It would also be helpful to give her as much silent independent reading time in the classroom as possible. Keyasia can sometimes get distracted easily when it comes to reading and writing, but with the right support I know that she is capable of learning and becoming an even more successful and experienced reader.

I hope that this letter provides you with useful and informative information about my tutoring sessions with Keyasia. I also sent a letter to Keyasia's mother informing her of the progress she has made over the past few months. In the short amount of time I have known Keyasia, I am very proud of the accomplishments she has with me and truly believe that she will only continue to succeed. Please feel free to contact me at any time with questions, comments, or suggestions.

Best,
Helen Wolf
Tutor at HC Literacy Space

Family Games Night

Time will also pass between the end of the first semester and the start of the second as the college will have a break between semesters, either from December until spring session in February or from May until September. It is critical not to lose the momentum of the work.

One way in which we help families both understand the diagnostic assessment and to continue supporting their child during the break is through Family Games Night. The goal of Family Games Night is invite parents into the Literacy Space room to join children and teachers in playing a variety of games, informally share stories, and celebrate the first semesters' progress.

In preparation for Family Games Night, teachers identify areas of literacy that they want to strengthen with their students. We share with them an article by Padak and Rasinski (2008) that describes 12 easy ways to make games that support phonemic awareness and decoding, sight-word identification, and vocabulary. Teachers make two or three of these games, write clear instructions, and play these games with the families during the Family Games Night. Teachers are able to tailor the games to the unique needs and interests of the child. For example, one teacher, knowing her student was a devoted NY Giants fan, used football pictures and team colors, in crafting her sight-word bingo game. As the families play the games, teachers are able to informally coach families as to the goals of the game and model responses. Families then can take the games home to share over the break between semesters. We discuss this further in chapter 10.

Family Workshops

In the second semester of Literacy Space, after teachers have learned much about their students and their families, we build upon those understandings, to further develop families' understandings of literacy development and support through family workshops. In class, we share questions and concerns families express about their children's reading, writing, and school experiences. Teachers brainstorm topic for workshops that will address the needs of the families. In groups of two or three, teachers collaborate to develop 45-minute workshops for families. A sample semester's series is below. We urge teachers to create interactive sessions, with hands-on experiences, and material to take home. We discuss these further in chapter 10.

Literacy Space Spring 2007 Family Workshops

March 19

- Trippin' in NYC: Reading Around the City March 26
- A Crash Course in Conferences April 16

• A Look Inside Today's Reading Classroom April 23
• Talking About TV, Talking About Books April 30
• Reading in Disguise

All workshops are from 4:45–5:45 p.m. while children are attending Literacy Space. All family members/caregivers welcome. Refreshments will be served.

The workshops are held in the waiting area next to Literacy Space. We work to ensure that translators are present, either teachers or other graduate students or family members to ensure all families can participate.

Reading Recital

After two semesters at Literacy Space, participating children develop a strong sense of pride and ownership in their accomplishments. Teachers, too, feel part of a strong community. As instructors, we believe it is important to honor and celebrate the accomplishments of children and teachers. Our Reading Recital is an opportunity for all participating children to publically share, in ways in which they are comfortable, their accomplishments in reading and writing. Many of the children who attend Literacy Space are not chosen to perform at their schools. For some children and families, the Reading Recital is the first time they have had a chance to be center stage.

In the weeks prior to the Reading Recital, teachers work with each other and their students to develop appropriate pieces for the recital.

Spring Reading Recital Program

Welcome	Jenny Tuten
Play Ball	Marcus Traversa
"Grandma's Beach"	Grace Williams
The Basketball Dilemma	Sanya Butto & Emma Jones
"A Rainy Day"	Tomas King
"Making Mud Cups"	Darnell Felix and Karlie Gomez
Time Flies	Abigail Ortega
Poem: Diamond	Zoe King
An Interview about Spiders	Emma Jones
Dolphin Book	Sara Marin
Dinosaur	Simon Marches
Selected Jokes	Charlie Green & Jack Levy
Polar Bears Grrr!	Jay Bruno & Esme Cortez
Sponge Bob and Patrick Watch T.V.	Eduardo Morales
Everybody's Reading!	Literacy Space Ensemble Awarding of Certificates

It is real-world opportunity to focus on reading fluency through the performance of poems, excerpts of books, Readers Theater, and jokes. Some students read or share stories, poems, or nonfiction texts that they have written themselves. What matters most is that all children have an opportunity to participate in the ways appropriate to their strengths.

We involve children and teachers in creating a program, invitations, refreshments, and decorations. On the evening of the Reading Recital, children and their families often bring relatives and friends along with cameras and video cameras. We rearrange the Literacy Space room to resemble a theater in the round. Children present alone, with a teacher, or in groups. Sometimes the entire group performs. Here is an example of a group composed chant:

Literacy Space Kids, Spring 2009
_____ is my name.
Reading is my game.
I like books about (that are)
That rhymes with _____.
Welcome to our final show
Into readers we did grow!
Before it's time for us to go,
Let us show you what we know!

Children had a chance to read their own name, provide a rhyme, and share a topic he or she likes to read about. All the children chorally read the second part of the chant. This was an opportunity for the children to demonstrate community and share their newfound excitement in reading.

Our Model of Reading

As we work with teachers, it is important for us to provide them with the support they need to develop a robust and research-based understanding of what it is to be a strong reader.

In the first of our two courses, we draw upon the work of McKenna and Stahl (2003/as a theoretical and practical infrastructure on which we develop our instruction. They posit a cognitive model of reading composed of three components: automatic word recognition, which we term "fluency," comprehension and language use, and strategic knowledge and use within texts. A strong or proficient reader would demonstrate grade appropriate abilities in all these areas. By selecting appropriate assessment tools, teachers can better understand

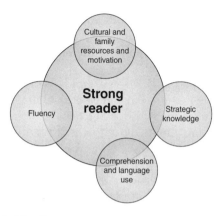

Figure 2.1   Model of Reading.

children's strengths and needs in each area. After working with this framework for the cognitive model of reading, we've adapted it to include the area of cultural and family background and support and motivation. These elements, in our experience, are integral in supporting readers. Figure 2.1 shows these elements.

Automatic word recognition, or fluency is a reader's ability to read aloud texts with ease and expression. One component of word recognition is phonological awareness, an ability to recognize and manipulate the discreet sounds that make up words. Another component is decoding ability—skill in recognizing the specific range of sounds letters and combinations of letters make in print and efficient ability to make recognize patterns in words. Sight-word ability is the skill in recognizing words, many in English, that are not decodable and so must be memorized. A fluent reader not only can decode familiar and unfamiliar words automatically but can also understand the connected text sufficiently in order to read with expression and comprehension. Putting all these skills together is reading fluency.

An equally important component of proficient reading is the ability to understand the language of the text. While some readers are able to decode or "word call" if they are unable to gain meaning from what has been read, they are struggling readers. Comprehension is an interconnected web of the meanings of words, vocabulary, and the ability to use knowledge of language and language structures to derive meaning. Reading comprehension depends on a reader's ability to move from making sense of the literal meaning of texts to understanding inferential references and synthesizing material.

Strategic knowledge is a reader's awareness of the their own reading process and purposes. Proficient readers understand and adapt their reading strategies in response to the variety of purposes for reading and demands of texts.

We've come to add cultural and family resources as a category because we believe in the social and emotional dimension of reading. A reader comes to us with his or her own background knowledge, shaped by their family and cultural experiences. We drew from the perspective of Culturally Responsive Teaching (CRT) as discussed by Gay (2000). This perspective argues that it is critical to use the cultural knowledge, experiences, and performance styles of diverse students in order to teach to their strengths. Equally important is the emphasis on bridging home and school experiences to strengthen students' learning.

Assessment at Literacy Space

The graduate courses, in which Literacy Space is embedded, each have a focus. The first, Assessment of Reading Difficulties, has an academic focus in honing teachers' abilities to understand, appropriately select and use, and finally analyze data from a wide variety of literacy assessments. This is the second course emphasizing assessment that teachers have had in this program. The previous course provides an overview of both informal and formal literacy assessment. We expect teachers to come to the Literacy Space work with a foundation of assessment knowledge but without having had the opportunity to put into action the assessments they've learned.

Because teachers have two semesters with one child, we are able to ask teachers to take time to get to know their tutee in depth. We believe that assessment is an ongoing, recursive process. That is, teachers use an assessment tool, analyze the data, plan and implement a teaching strategy, and then reassess. We also believe it is important to use multiple assessments to draw meaningful conclusions about students' abilities and needs.

Sometimes data from assessments conflict and so it is important for teachers to dig beneath the tools in order to get a deeper understanding of a child's literacy behaviors. As you read the opening and closing profiles of each struggling reader you will see this in action.

As part of the course we've developed a collection of core assessments that all teachers use with their children. These assessments, both informal and formal, tap into the critical components of proficient reading, as discussed in the earlier section. We require all

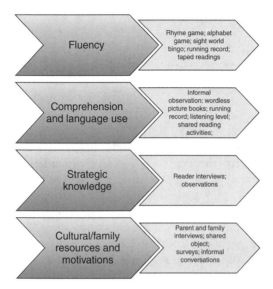

Figure 2.2   Reading Domains.

teachers to use these tools to develop a diagnostic profile of their student. These core assessment tools provide teachers with preliminary information in each of the four components of proficient reading as we defined earlier. Figure 2.2 demonstrates this. As teachers discover the particular strengths and needs of their student, they identify specific areas of literacy that they see need further investigation. This is where we challenge teachers to use their prior knowledge of literacy development to use the assessment data to make further decisions as to what to do next. Here, we present a brief overview of the core assessments and then return to their use in practice in the following chapters. The patterns of struggling readers we will discuss in chapters 3–8 emerged from this process.

Core Assessments

The following are the core assessments we require teachers to use with students in order to develop a comprehensive profile of their reading abilities.

- Shared object
- Wordless picture books
- Informal observations

- Running record
- Listening level
- Informal Reading Inventory (IRI)
- Phonemic awareness and decoding activities
- Interest and strategy inventories
- Interviews

Shared Objects

Before children arrive at Literacy Space, they receive a letter of introduction from their teachers. Each teacher writes a letter to the girl or the boy she will be tutoring. At this stage, the teacher knows only the child's name, age, and grade in school. In the letter, we suggest teachers share something about themselves and tell a bit about what will be going on in Literacy Space. Teachers also ask the children to bring to the first session an object from home that is important to the child. We ask teachers to also bring in a special object for the first tutoring session. One of the instructors brings in her charm bracelet to share with the teachers to illustrate this idea. Whenever she travels, she purchases a charm for her bracelet as a remembrance or souvenir of her trip. She

Figure 2.3   Charm Bracelet.

Dear Molly,
We are going to have fun together at Literacy Space. On the first day bring one of your favorite things to show me.
Your tutor,
Karen

Figure 2.4   Letter to Student.

explains to the class how special the bracelet has become, and when she wears it the charms remind her of the wonderful times she has spent with her husband and son over the years (see figure 2.3).

It is important to us that the children coming to their first tutoring session bring something from home. Coming to a new situation can be frightening, especially for children who may have had negative experiences with school. The letter and the shared object is a first step in building community. Children and teachers are on more equal ground as they take turns talking about the objects. These initial conversations provide useful information for the teachers. Through listening and afterward recording anecdotal notes, teachers are able to document an initial assessment of children's oral abilities and their preferences. The letter below is a sample sent to a young child two weeks before beginning our program (see figure 2.4).

Wordless Picture Books

Wordless picture books encourage language use. They provide the framework for storytelling and a window into the child's understanding of literacy-related activities such as concept of story, sequence of events, and use of prior knowledge. We have used wordless picture books with all of our struggling readers but especially with those children who struggle with English. A further discussion of wordless picture books and how to use them with struggling readers can be found in chapter 6.

Informal Observations

"Kidwatching" is a term coined by Goodman et al. (1987) to describe carefully watching a child's reading and writing behaviors in a variety of contexts. Instead of checking behaviors off on a list, "kidwatching" anecdotal records provide richer, contextualized descriptions of what children are doing as they read and write. We ask teachers to document their observations of children during both the assessment and, most importantly, the community time activities. This provides the opportunity for ongoing informal assessment in authentic situations.

Running Record

A running record is a written transcription and then coding of a reader's recitation of a text. It is a way to look at a reader's oral performance in order to gain insight into a reader's strategies and behaviors. This tool was originally developed by Marie Clay (1993) but is similar to procedures used in informal reading inventories (discussed below) and the Reading Miscue procedures (Goodman, Watson, and Burke, 1987; Wilde, 2000).

In running record assessments, students are asked to read a short story or nonfiction text aloud, while the teacher documents the student's reading noting the number of words read correctly, the attempts the reader makes at words, and the strategies the reader uses while reading. It provides evidence of a reader's decoding abilities and can also be used to determine what level of text is appropriate for the reader.

Listening Level

In developing a profile of a struggling reader it is important to determine if difficulties in comprehension are related to decoding issues or to language issues. A listening level is defined as the highest level of text comprehended by a reader who can answer 75 percent of questions about the text after listening to it read aloud (McKenna and Stahl, 2003). "The listening level provides an estimate of the student's immediate potential for reading improvement" (Gillet et al., 2008). It is not absolute but provides a guideline to use in conjunction with other observational information as well as interests about the student.

The listening level indicates whether the student has the potential to improve as a reader. Johns (2008) suggested, "When a substantial difference exists between the student's instructional level and listening level [generally a year or more], it usually indicates that the student should be able to make significant growth in reading achievement with appropriate instruction" (p. 10). It assists teachers in setting reasonable goals for the student since they can determine what they can expect the student to achieve. As reading improves, the listening level also rises.

The key to developing a listening level is to immerse the student in a rich language environment (Gillet et al., 2008). The student must be read to since during initial read-alouds students gain their first concepts of story and get a sense of how story language differs from talk. Jennings and colleagues (2006) claim that struggling readers benefit from listening to teachers read by absorbing rich language, learning how a story is organized, and have the opportunity to build background knowledge.

Knowing the listening level of the child assists the tutor in selecting books to use with the struggling reader. When selecting books within this targeted area, the tutor can be assured that the child will be successful in comprehending the text. The listening level can be found using comprehension passages of an informal reading inventory.

IRIs

IRIs are reading assessments designed to provide a picture of a reader's reading abilities. Usually they consist of graded or leveled reading lists and passages or short books. Typically, the teacher begins with the word lists that would give the teacher a general idea of where to begin the student in the longer texts. The reading of the list also provides information about the student's decoding abilities. After reading the leveled or graded passages, and assessing comprehension through retelling and questioning, the teacher then can determine an instructional level for the student. There are many commercially available IRIs, such as Qualitative Reading Inventory (Leslie and Caldwell, 2005), Roe and Burns Informal Reading Inventory (Roe and Burns, 2005), or Applegate, Quinn, and Applegate (2004).

Phonemic Awareness and Decoding Activities

While some aspects of phonemic awareness and decoding and word-level abilities are assessed through the running record and IRI assessments, it is also important to gain more detailed information about students' decoding abilities that match what the teacher has observed in earlier assessments. Rather than give all students the same assessments, we ask teachers to look at the data collected in the informal observations and running records to determine what additional assessments would be useful.

Some children exhibit difficulty distinguishing differences in the sounds of letters and words, and so assessments of phonemic awareness is necessary. Teachers use poems and nursery rhymes to assess knowledge of rhyme, ability to segment words and put together words with sounds.

To assess phonics knowledge, blocks and word games are used to assess children's abilities to decode.

For younger readers, assessment of alphabet knowledge is accomplished through play with magnetic letters, word stamps, and environmental print.

Interest and Strategy Inventories

In order to successfully work with struggling readers, it is critical that we tap into their interests. To learn even more about children's interest, teachers use a variety of interest inventories to elicit information about the areas children care about and may prove to be sources of materials for future lessons. Completing these inventories, too, is another way for teacher and student to get to know each other and build trust.

Additionally, it is important for teachers to understand how their students understand and view reading. Samples of interest and attitude inventories can be found at the back of this chapter.

Interviews

One critical component of the core assessment process is an interview with each child's family. We use a structured interview form, to support all teachers in gaining information, but encourage teachers to listen carefully and follow up with questions.

We use the interview to both gain information and establish a two-way dialogue between family and teacher. These are discussed in chapter 10.

Developing a Profile and an Annotated Bibliography

At the end of the first semester, teachers have completed, at minimum, the core assessments discussed above. We ask them now to create a rich profile that describes and documents their student as a person, family and community member, and literacy learner. These profile incorporate summaries of each assessment and a synthesis of the information to form a plan or a roadmap for the following semester's intervention plan.

In addition, we ask teachers to create an annotated bibliography of texts and materials to use in support of the tutoring plans. It is critical, as research (Mesmer, 2008) supports, for struggling readers to work with text that are accessible to them, that is, match their instructional reading level, and engage their interests and imagination. Many teachers have had few opportunities to research and select texts to support specific learners. This assignment challenges teachers to research texts and other materials, analyze them carefully, and think about how to purposely use them in lesson planning. Below is an example that illustrates the purposeful selection of texts.

Annotated Bibliography

1. *Kitten Likes to Play*
   Written by: Bruce Larkin
   Wilbooks – Books For A Cause, Inc.
   2003
   Text Description: Kitten has many adventures during the night while everyone is asleep. In the end, we find out what happens to the kitten when everyone wakes up.
   Rationale: This book is a level G, which is Mathew's current guided reading level. I chose this book based upon conversations and interest inventories where he spoke about both his pet cat and other people's cats. It is a book that I can use either for an informal reading inventory, or for a retelling activity, encouraging Mathew to focus on specific details in the story.

2. *Hi Fly, Guy*
   Written by Tedd Arnold
   Scholastic, Inc.
   2005
   Text Description: A boy chooses a fly as a pet and attempts to win the "Amazing Pet Show." The judges are skeptical at first, however, that quickly changes when the fly's performance amazes them all.
   Rationale: I chose this book, first, because it is at the guided reading level H, which is one level above Mathew's current reading level. I also chose this book because it is divided into chapters and I wanted to use a few chapter books with Mathew, instead of only using picture books, in an attempt to boost his confidence. Through using a variety of strategies, for example, echo reading, I will use this book to scaffold Mathew's reading level.

3. *Trouble at the Bridge*
   Written by: Marie Birkinshaw
   Dorling KIngersley Publishing, Inc.
   2000
   Text Description: In Lego city, a new City Bridge is being built. This book tells about how everyone helps. It also tells what they do to solve problems that are preventing the bridge from being built.
   Rationale: Mathew loves legos! I chose this book to bridge his interest of lego-building with reading. Although this book is at a guided reading level I, it could be used as a read-aloud, keeping Mathew engaged by activating prior knowledge and making predictions.

4. *Oh My Gosh, Mrs. McNosh!*
   Written by: Sarah Weeks
   Scholastic, Inc.
   2002
   Text Description: Mrs. McNosh's dog, George, starts chasing a squirrel while on a walk through the park. Mrs. McNosh loses her hold on George and begins chasing him through the park. She encounters many different obstacles before finally giving up and returning home, where she finds George waiting for her at the door.
   Rationale: This book is a level H, one level above Mathew's current guided reading level, but also includes rhyming and repetitive text patterns. Mathew has expressed to me his dislike and difficulty with rhyming, so this humorous book about a dog that runs away could be used to make predictions, using the rhyming words as clues.

Using the annotated bibliography and the instructional goals, teachers develop lesson that address the particular literacy needs of their students. As discussed in chapter 1, our goal for teachers is to develop their professional abilities to plan instruction based on assessments and to incorporate structure and creativity in that planning. Our suggested lesson plan format supports that (see Appandix 2-E).

Summary

In this chapter, we highlighted the innovations we have made in the Literacy Space program. We've shared our framework and general tools for assessment and the development and structure of an intervention plan. In the following chapters, we look more deeply at profiles of struggling readers and the particular tools and strategies that successfully support their literacy growth. We provide the research that underlies our understandings, assessment choices, and intervention plans.

References

Applegate, M. D., Quinn, K. B., and Applegate, A. J. (2004). *The Critical Reading Inventory*. Upper Saddle River, NJ: Prentice Hall.

Clay, M. (1993). *Reading Recovery: A Guidebook for Teachers in Training*. Portsmouth, NH: Heinemann.

Gay, G. (2000). *Culturally Responsive Teaching: Theory, Research, and Practice*. New York: Teachers College Press.

Gillet, J. W., Temple, C., and Crawford, A. (2008). *Understanding Reading Problems: Assessment and Instruction*. 7th ed. Boston, MA: Pearson.

Goodman, Y. M., Watson, D. J., and Burke, C. L. (1987). *Reading Miscue Inventory: Alternate Procedures*. New York: Richard Owens.

Jennings, J. H., Caldwell, J., and Lerner, J. W. (2006). *Reading Problems: Assessment and Teaching Strategies*. 5th ed. Boston, MA: Pearson.

Johns, J. L. (2008). *Basic Inventory*. 10th ed. Dubuque, IA: Kendall/Hunt Publishing Company.

Leslie, L. and Caldwell, J. S. (2005). *Qualitative Reading Inventory-4*. New York: Allyn Bacon.

McKenna, M. C. and Stahl, S. (2003). *Assessment for Reading Instruction*. New York: Guilford Press.

Mesmer, H. (2008). *Tools for Matching Readers to Texts: Research Based Practices*. New York: Guilford Press.

Padak, N. and Rasinski, T. (2008). "The games children play." *The Reading Teacher*, 62(4): 363–365.

Roe, B. and Burns, P. (2005). *Informal Reading Inventory, Preprimer to 12 Grade*. New York: Wandsworth.

Wilde, S. (2000). *Miscue Analysis Made Easy: Building on Student Strengths*. Portsmouth, NH: Heinemann.

Appendix 2-A Smiley Face Reading Attitude Survey

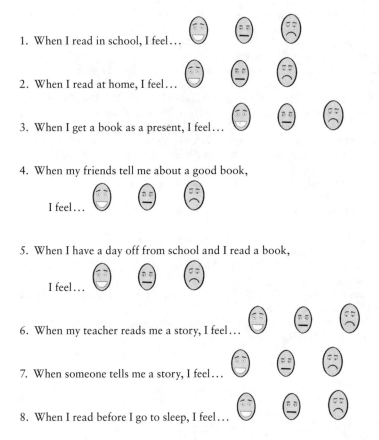

1. When I read in school, I feel...

2. When I read at home, I feel...

3. When I get a book as a present, I feel...

4. When my friends tell me about a good book,
   I feel...

5. When I have a day off from school and I read a book,
   I feel...

6. When my teacher reads me a story, I feel...

7. When someone tells me a story, I feel...

8. When I read before I go to sleep, I feel...

Appendix 2-B   Interest Inventory

1. What do you like to do with your free time?

2. What kind of games do you like to play?

3. Do you like to collect anything?

4. What are your favorite television shows?

5. What is the name of your favorite book that someone read aloud to you?

6. Do you play any sports?

7. If you could meet any famous person from the present or the past, who would it be?

8. What is your favorite food to eat?

9. If you could turn into any animal, what would you be?

10. Do you take any lessons such as music, dancing?

11. Do you read magazines?

12. What is your favorite subject in school?

Appendix 2-C   Reading Attitude Survey Checklist

	Always	Sometimes	Never
I enjoy reading books for fun			
I enjoy reading books for school			
I enjoy sharing books with friends			
I have a favorite author/series			
I think reading is hard			
It takes me a long time to read a book			
I go to the library to borrow books			
I read before I go to sleep			
I like having books read to me			
I like learning new words			
I like to read magazines			
I like to read comic books			
Books make good presents			
I finish the books I start to read			
Reading books is boring			

Complete the following sentences:

My favorite subject in school is _____.

The best book is _____.

After school I usually _____.

On Saturdays I usually _____.

Appendix 2-D   If I Ran This School Interest Inventory

If ran
the school

A PRIMARY
INTEREST
INVENTORY
developed by
Deborah E. Burns
designed by Del Siegle

Name _____

Grade _____   Teacher _____

If I ran the school, I would choose to learn about these ten things.
I have thought about my answers very carefully and I have
circled my best ideas for right now.

I am really interested in:

1. The Stars and Planets
2. Birds
3. Dinosaurs and Fossils
4. Life in the Ocean
5. Trees, Plants and Flowers
6. The Human Body
7. Monsters and Mysteries
8. Animals and Their Homes
9. Outer Space, Astronauts, and Rockets
10. The Weather
11. Electricity, Light, and Energy
12. Volcanoes and Earthquakes
13. Insects
14. Reptiles
15. Rocks and Minerals
16. Machines and Engines
17. Diseases and Medicine
18. Chemistry and Experiments

1. Families
2. The Future
3. Our Presidents
4. The United States
5. Other Countries
6. History and Long Ago Times
7. Famous Men and Women
8. Problems We Have in Our Town
9. Holidays
10. Native Americans, Asian Americans, Hispanics and African Americans
11. Explorers
12. People Who Live and Work in Our Town
13. Travel and Transportation

1. Math Games and Puzzlers
2. Measuring Lines, Liquids, Weight
3. Shapes and Sizes
4. Buying and Money
5. Calculators and Computers
6. Building
7. Counting and Numbering
8. Calendars and Time
9. Math Stories and Problems

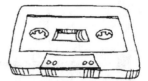

1. Writing a Book
2. Writing Poems
3. Writing Plays and Skits
4. Writing Newspapers
5. Making Speeches
6. Sign Language
7. Making a Book
8. Comic and Cartoon Strips
9. Letter Writing
10. Spanish and French
11. Talking and Listening to Stories
12. Making a New Game or Puzzle

1. Cartoons
2. Art Projects
3. Painting
4. Clay
5. Acting
6. Dancing
7. Drawing
8. Writing Music
9. Photography
10. Movies
11. Puppets
12. Radio and Television
13. Famous Artists and Their Work
14. Making New Toys
15. Magic
16. Mime

1. Doctors
2. Lawyers
3. Police Work
4. Fire Fighters
5. Scientists
6. Builders
7. Reporters
8. Store Worker
9. Sports Stars
10. Actors
11. Veterinarian
12. Farmers
13. Writers
14. Engineers
15. Artists
16. Inventors

You forgot to list some of my very special interests. They are: _____

Appendix 2-E   Lesson Plan Template

Lesson Plan #
Child's Name:

Literacy Needs Addressed:
Texts Used:
Other Materials:
Activities:
Links to Future Lessons:

Souta, an English Language Learner

Souta sat with his mother and his brother outside Literacy Space waiting anxiously for his tutor. He and Takahiro were both coming to Literacy Space for the first time. Souta, age six, and Takahiro, age eight, sat quietly clutching the letter they each received from their tutors two weeks earlier. They would occasionally whisper to their mom in Japanese. Souta lives at home with his brother, mother, and father. Although Souta's father is fluent in English, Japanese is the language of the home and the only language his mother speaks.

Souta looked tentatively at Andi, his tutor, when she came out to greet him and to welcome him into our classroom. He looked back at his brother and walked slowly with Andi to a table in the corner. They chatted about the special objects they each brought in as an icebreaker for a while. Souta brought in a collection of Legos© in a plastic bag and began showing Andi how to put them together to create some of his favorite superheroes. However, Souta never looked comfortable until Takahiro and his tutor Lizzy joined them. Andi and Lizzy decided to expand on the boys' interest in superheroes using some of the puzzles in Literacy Space. They worked on Spiderman puzzles together, all four chatting away about the adventures of Spiderman from movies they had seen. Andi found an *I Spy* book featuring Batman and his various nemeses. Reading aloud from the clues, Andi and Lizzy were observing to see if the boys understood what the clues were asking them to find hidden in the detailed illustrations in the book. They were trying to determine the extent of the boys' vocabulary in the context of an *I Spy* book about a favorite subject.

Souta attends first grade in an urban public school. He receives English as Second Language (ESL) services in a pullout program at his school. He was born in the United States, speaks Japanese at home and English at school. His teacher referred him to Literacy Space.

As the session continued, it was clear to Andi that Souta had only a beginning knowledge of English, finding it difficult to find the right words to describe his school experiences, his home life, and things of his interest during their informal conversations. She suspected that his emergent English proficiency was the reason the school had recommended Souta to our program. She also knew that there is not one profile for all English Language Learners (ELLs) or one response adequate enough to meet their educational goals and needs. Andi was curious to find out what other interests Souta had and how she could use them in her assessment and intervention plans. As she filled in her first Daily Record of Activities Sheet, she carefully planned the interest and attitude surveys she would use and some of the games she might play with him during community time to assist her in discovering Souta's interests, strengths, and areas in need of additional instruction.

Research on ELLs

There is an increase of ELLs in our classrooms. The number of school-age children, age 5–17, who spoke a language other than English at home rose from 4.7 to 11.2 million between 1980 and 2009 (National Center for Education Statistics, 2011). This represents an increase from 10 percent to 21 percent of the population within this age range. In 2011, the National Center for Education Statistics (NCES) also reported that among the school-age children who spoke non-English language at home, the percentage of who spoke English with difficulty generally decreased during the same time period while the school enrollment increased from 90 percent to 93 percent. In fact, 79 percent of children in immigrant families were born in the United States and 64 percent of immigrant families have one parent who is a US citizen either naturalized or US born (Hernandez et al., 2008).

However, NCES (2011) was careful to note that these findings varied by demographic characteristics including race/ethnicity, citizenship status, poverty status, and the child's age noting that the US born, older the child will have less difficulty with English. Similarly, the National Council of Teachers of English (2008) reminded us that there is no one profile of an ELL student or one single response to meet the student's educational goals or needs. Many have a deep sense of the non-US culture, multiple cultures, or with the US culture only.

Some children live in cultural enclaves and while other children are surrounded by English-speaking families. Each child learning English falls at a different point of the spectrum. Students who can already read and write in their native language have an easier time adjusting to school in which English is spoken most of the time (Bear et al., 2003). In their longitudinal study, August et al., (2006), found that first language reading skills are directly related to a student's second-language reading skills. Their findings suggest that children must have the first language literacy skill for the relationship even to exist.

As the percentage of school-age children who are ELLs grows, only 33 states have teacher standards for ELL instruction (National Center for Education Statistics, 2011). Many schools are not prepared to respond to the increase of ELLs joining their classrooms. They also report that Arizona, Florida, and New York are the only states that require all prospective teachers to demonstrate competence in ELL instruction. Eleven states offer teachers incentives to earn ESL licensure and/or endorsement, and seven states ban or restrict native language instruction in their public schools. Most teachers must rely on prior college course learning, the current culture of the school and its attitude toward ELL instruction, or take the initiative to research and learn effective instructional strategies on their own. In schools using a scripted program with little to no ELL instructional accommodations, teachers find it difficult to deliver appropriate instruction to their ELLs. Finding time to provide effective instruction is also a challenge for many teachers. Teachers must learn to reach out to the resident ESL teachers for assistance in planning and implementing effective instruction and the schools need to provide time for these collaborative efforts.

It may seem obvious then that ELLs are one of the largest groups of students who struggle with literacy (Hickman et al., 2004). Yet, this group of struggling readers and writers is highly diverse and the teacher is challenged to meet the varying needs of the children who are ELLs. Teachers are concerned about how best to help the increasing numbers of ELLs succeed (Ogle and Correa-Kovtun, 2010). "The challenge for schools, then, is to accelerate English mastery so that students with immigrant backgrounds can excel in academic subjects, ideally while retaining fluency in their heritage language" (Tienda, 2008, p. 16). The type of language that is necessary for school success, referred to as Academic English, is difficult to master since it is rarely used outside the classroom (Goldenberg, 2008). "Academic language has longer sentences, more complex grammar and more technical vocabulary than social language" (Bursuck and Damer, 2007, p. 291). So how do teachers identify best strategies that best work with such a diverse population of struggling readers and writers?

Although we advocate that teachers assess the needs within their ELL student population, research suggests that there are some common strategies for assisting children who are learning English. Goldenberg (2008) suggests that effective second-language instruction include both explicit teaching that helps students directly learn the features of the second language and ample opportunity to use the second language in meaningful and motivating situations. Small-group interventions, regular peer-assisted learning, close monitoring, extensive and varied vocabulary instruction are among the strategies that improve effectiveness of literacy learning for ELLs (Gersten et al., 2007). "English learners who are engaged in and contributing to the learning process will remember more, be able to apply their learning, and show teachers if and where confusion exists," (Helman et al., 2012, p. 63). When given a separate block of time dedicated to oral English proficiency, students scored higher on proficiency tests and Saunders and colleagues (2006) claimed this result was because teachers used the time more efficiently and focused their use of time effectively. Taking these general suggestions into consideration, teachers can also adapt the following findings into their instructional practices when working with ELL children.

We do offer this caveat: it is important to recognize that some of the usual assessments teachers use with their students to discover their literacy strengths and areas of need may not be appropriate for ELLs. Phonemic awareness and phonics tests, some parts of the Informal Reading Inventory (IRI), and vocabulary measures may yield unreliable results (Vogt and Shearer, 2007). Data suggest that oral language proficient in English, although important for assessment, may not be a reliable indicator of reading difficulties in the early grades (Lovett et al., 2008). The phonology of the student's native language may be completely different from the English language that some of the sounds may be indistinguishable or difficult to reproduce by some ELLs. "Additionally, a problem can occur when students are assessed using formats that they are unfamiliar with because these formants do not exist in the schools in their home countries" (Brantley, 2007 p. 32).

Teachers need to help children learning English to see their native languages and family culture as resources to contribute to their education rather than something to overcome or cast aside (National

Council of Teachers of English, 2008). They need stories to reflect their culture and experience to support their comprehension (Ganske et al., 2003). Goldenberg (2008) reported that according to the National Literacy Panel, when ELLs read texts with more familiar material such as stories with themes and content from their own culture, their comprehension improves.

Teachers need to find out the children's interests. "Interest fosters persistence and a desire to understand, while topic knowledge supports children's word identification and comprehension by enabling them to draw on what they know" (Ganske et al., 2003). It is important to find text that matches to the student's interests and reading level. It is interest and background knowledge that allows students to read beyond what is considered normal reading level. ELLs frequently do not have the necessary background knowledge to understand text. Slang, idioms, background of US customs, and special demands of nonfiction make it difficult for ELL students to comprehend text (Ganske et al., 2003; Ogle and Correa-Kovtun, 2010; Rasinski et al., 2010). Activating and drawing upon the students' background knowledge is an important aid to comprehension and vocabulary (Hickman et al., 2004).

The best instruction in reading for ELL students indicates that the very same research-based factors identified for English-speaking students work well (Rasinski et al., 2010). Yet, according to Lenters (2004/2005), what is unique to second-language learners in becoming literate in English is the sound/symbol dissimilarity or interference, oral vocabulary constraints, limitations due to insufficient background knowledge, and difficulties with text structure. In a four-year study of ELLs and English first learners, Lovett and her colleagues (2008) claimed that the same principals of systematic and explicit phonologically based instruction are effective for both groups of struggling readers. No matter the first language, struggling readers demonstrated growth in word and test reading as well as growth in phonological processing.

In addition, most ELL students need to be given increased academic learning time, increased time for reading, opportunity to use language, and small-group interventions so that students have extended time to participate in discussions, varied and extensive vocabulary instruction, and opportunities for peer-assisted literacy learning, yet there is a gap between what is known and what is implemented when instructing in classrooms with ELL students (Ganske et al., 2003; Garcia et al., 2009). The ELL may need more time to process academic language and concepts, requiring teachers to give more wait time for responses (Verma et al., 2008). Significant growth occurs when intervention includes phonemic awareness, letter knowledge, alphabetic decoding, decodable text practice, and comprehension strategies (Vaughn et al., 2006).

Knowing less English made it harder to learn additional English according to Goldenberg's review of the research (2008), which is one reason why vocabulary development is so important for the ELLs. Teachers need to weave rich vocabulary-oriented activities throughout the daily instruction, providing explicit instruction using semantically rich words, child-friendly definitions, an appreciation for words (Manyak and Bauer, 2009), opportunity to practice learning words and conscious attention to glossaries in nonfiction texts (Ogle and Correa-Kovtun, 2010), explicit instruction in basic vocabulary that is hard to visualize (Hickman et al., 2004), and using words of high utility across content areas (Beck et al., 2002). Second-language vocabulary acquisition is an extremely important predictor of second-language reading comprehension (August et al., 2006).

Vocabulary growth can occur indirectly through language exposure and not necessarily from direct instruction (Lenters, 2004/2005). Yet, ongoing, direct vocabulary instruction will improve the ELL students' oral language skills and the students increased oral language skills allows for more extended discussion and opportunity to learn new words (Goldenberg, 2008; Hickman et al., 2004; Lenters, 2004/2005). "ELLs learn more words when the words are embedded in meaningful contexts and students are provided with ample opportunities for their repetition and use, as opposed to looking up dictionary definitions or presenting words in simple sentences" (Goldenberg, 2008, p. 17).

Some of the suggestions for successful reading instruction for ELL students include an increased time spent conversing and gaining an oral vocabulary. Prereading activities to scaffold vocabulary development and using illustrations to talk about the reading should be included. Reading materials should include 90–95 percent known words to the child with opportunity to reread the text and authentic activities to respond to text. Simple, predictable texts, books on tape, culturally relevant stories are important for literacy development. Brantley (2007) stated that it is imperative to use quality literature with ELLs in order to provide exemplary models of the English language while engaging them in appealing stories. Teachers should utilize retellings, guided reading, and QAR and DRTA strategies to enhance meaningful instruction (Brantley, 2007; Hickman, et al., 2004; Lenters, 2004/2005). Using language experience approach, sometimes called dictated texts, are a great bridge from oral to written language (Rasinski et al., 2010), and are wonderful vehicles for teaching ELLs. Koskinen and colleagues (1999) found having ELL students use books and records for reading practice resulted in reading achievement and interest as well as self-confidence.

Background Tools Used with Souta

Andi knew the key to working successfully with Souta would have to begin with finding his interests. She also knew that the tools she needed to select should not challenge Souta's beginning English proficiency. She wanted to get to know him without causing him to be frustrated or anxious. She chose to use his Special Object, If I Ran This School, and the Smiley Face Reading Attitude Survey.

Souta brought in Batman Legos© that he enjoyed playing with at home. He explained he had a large collection of them at home and the ones in the baggie were just a small part the many he owned. Although Batman was his current favorite, he had other superheroes, pirates, and cars. He was very quick to put them together having done so many times before. Fortunately, Andi found both a puzzle of Spiderman and an I Spy book of Batman to extend her first session with Souta and engage him in something of which he was interested. She noted on her Daily Record of Activity Sheet that he seemed quick to settle in, seemed to have a lot of energy, and he enjoyed the puzzle and book about a superhero. She was curious to find other interest and wondered how he felt about other books. She planned to use an interest inventory during their next session together.

If I Ran This School is an interest inventory developed by Deborah E. Burns and designed by Del Siegle, and can be found at the back of chapter 2. Souta selected animals, building, comic and cartoon strips, making a new game or puzzle, and art projects as he and Andi went through the lists on the interest inventory. She felt these were consistent with her first impressions of Souta during their initial session.

Using the Smiley Face Reading Attitude Survey, Andi found that Souta enjoys hearing stories and having books read to him. He circled all the unhappy faces when the questions asked how he felt about books and reading in school. In some cases, Andi was unsure if he understood the questions so discounted some of his responses.

Andi was impressed by the energy Souta brought to Literacy Space especially when using games and other interactive materials during their sessions. She knew she wanted her assessments to be quick and efficient, giving her the most information in the smallest amount of time so not to interfere or deter Souta's enthusiasm. She wanted to keep the majority of their time together to be unlike his school experiences that made him unhappy.

Assessment Tools Used with Souta

By using carefully selected background tools, Andi learned several of Souta's strengths and areas where he might need additional assistance. She immediately became aware of his emergent understanding and use of English. She also noticed that he demonstrated a positive attitude toward reading while listening to stories, but was not using the illustrations to understand the story. She wanted to be able to select books that she knew he would understand. She wanted to know the extent of his vocabulary, what control of the English language he did have, and what word-attack strategies he owned. She knew that with any assessment she would have to make sure Souta knew how to respond in the way the assessment required. The following assessment tools were the ones that Andi chose to use with Souta: IRI to determine listening level, sight-word lists, and a running record. She also used the Group Reading Assessment and Diagnostic Evaluation (GRADE) as a standardized instrument.

IRI

Andi used an IRI to determine Souta's listening comprehension level and discovered it to be a full grade above his current first-grade level. Since Japanese is his first language and the language spoken at home, his opportunities for English have been limited to his interactions at his public school. It appeared that Souta could understand most of the oral instruction at school and conversations with his classmates. Souta enjoyed having stories read to him and could comprehend when on grade level. Andi felt confident in selecting from a wide range of books to read to him during their sessions together.

Sight-Word Lists

Using graded sight-word lists, Andi began with a prefirst-grade list. Souta was able to identify 90 percent of the words on the beginning list indicating that books at this level would be in Souta's independent reading level. When she utilized the first-grade list, Souta's current grade in school, he was able to identify 75 percent of the words on the list that would indicate that the books at this level would be at his instructional level. Andi didn't feel that she needed to assess Souta's sight-word recognition with other lists or to continue until she found his frustration level. She felt that with repeated readings, sight-word bingo games, and word study at an appropriate level, Souta's sight-word recognition would naturally increase.

Word Study

Souta was learning vowel sounds and consonant digraphs in English that are completely different than in Japanese. Souta struggled with vowel sounds and consonant digraphs. One of his spelling inventories taken from *Words Their Way with English Learners*, 2nd Edition (2012) is given in figure 3.1. Souta's initial sounds are correct, yet, he does not own many of the short vowel sounds and blends. This did not concern Andi since she felt that Souta's classmates who were English first learners and also struggling would be having similar difficulties.

Figure 3.1 Souta's Spelling Assessment

Souta did represent initial, medial, and ending sounds that he heard in words. Andi found this encouraging.

1. fan
2. pet
3. dig
4. rob
5. hope
6. wait
7. gum
8. sled
9. stick
10. shine
11. dream
12. blade
13. coach
14. fright
15. thorn

Knowing this information, Andi was curious to find out what Souta was able to read himself and decided to employ a running record.

Running Record

When Andi began to complete running records, Souta was not using picture clues to reinforce his understanding of text or to apply words to pictures. He did not self-correct when he miscued. His vocabulary was not rich when it came to reading the books employed during a running record; however, when she completed running records with books on topics of his interest or awareness, his reading fell into an independent level. Souta read haltingly and Andi decided that he would benefit from participating in choral and shared reading and considered using books on tape with which Souta could read along.

GRADE

GRADE is a reading test that determines the developmental skills a student has mastered and where the student needs additional instruction. It also helps teachers plan instruction. The GRADE has levels PreK through grade 12. It is usually given to groups of children at one time. It is norm-referenced.

We use it in Literacy Space as a standardized assessment tool. It has different parts to assess word reading, listening and reading comprehension, and has early literacy skills included in the early levels of the test. We usually use only the selected parts of the GRADE with different students. We prefer to give it untimed, an option included with the GRADE, and will repeat questions to students when there is a need. Since the test is designed to be flexible, no special accommodations are specifically recommended for the ELLs. The manual indicates that it is appropriate to read the questions to the students twice and to allow enough time for students to mark their answers. These are some of the aspects of the assessment tool that are attractive to us.

Andi used level 1, equated to first grade, with Souta. She decided to use the passage comprehension portion of the GRADE since she had already determined a listening level using and IRI and had employed word lists prior to the GRADE. During the administration of the GRADE, she found it difficult to get him to focus on multiple-choice assessment without having to read each question aloud to him and giving him constant reinforcement to continue on. He did strive for the right answer and continued to ask for positive reinforcement. He struggled with word placement.

Souta's Literacy Profile

Andi found that Souta was able to focus his attention during the various assessments she employed to determine his strengths and areas in need of intervention. He brought with him an enthusiasm and energy to each session that Andi felt she could channel into their work. He was able to match words to pictures slowly when assessing his vocabulary but did not use picture clues to help him with unknown words when reading text. He was able to answer questions about what was read to him.

She also found that Souta needed to repeat questions and/or words out loud several times during assessments and took a long time to match words to pictures; he was correct but it was not immediate. She also discovered that he had difficulties putting together sentences with correct words. Many of his responses to questions were not correct in content; however, he did choose words that could have been correct if the sentence had been arranged differently. He used words from the questions, but used them in an incorrect order or in a way that did not make sense, common in ELLs when their first language' syntax is different from the syntax of English.

Souta had clear interests, enjoyed being read to, and was able to hear sounds of words in the beginning, medial, and ending positions although he struggled with long and short vowel sounds and digraphs. Using words lists at the first-grade level, Souta was at an instructional level. His listening level indicated that individualized intervention could bring him up to grade level.

Souta's Strengths

- Ability to match pictures to words.
- Listening level above grade level.
- Comprehension at primer level.
- Ability to hear beginning, medial, and ending sounds in words.
- Enthusiastic learner.

Souta's Vulnerabilities

- Struggles with some long and short vowel sounds.
- Struggles with digraphs.
- Not comprehending grade-level text.
- Small automatic sight-word recognition.
- Beginning vocabulary knowledge.
- Short attention span.

Intervention and Instructional Plans for Souta

Andi put together five instructional goals for Souta:

- Increase sight-word recognition.
- Develop a larger working vocabulary.
- Develop decoding ability for long and short vowels.
- Develop word family knowledge.
- Increase comprehension of text.

To increase sight-word recognition:

- Use highlighting tape during reading.
- Play sight-word bingo.
- Sight-word Slap Game.

To develop a larger working vocabulary:

- Implement rich instructional conversations around books.
- Use community-time activities to promote oral language such as Guess Who© and Riddle Maze©.
- Use picture sorts.

To develop decoding strategies:

- Use trade books specified for vowel sounds.
- Implement word sorts around vowel sounds.
- Play and Learn Phonics Game©.

To develop word family knowledge:

- Word family puzzle library.
- Word sorts.
- Use magnetic letters.

To increase comprehension of text:

- Repeated readings.
- Retellings with flannel pieces.
- Use Little Critter books by M. Mayer.

Andi loved Souta's enthusiasm and energy. She wanted to keep him engaged and knew he had a short attention span. She put together a collection of books from which she could do word sorts, reinforce word knowledge with games, do crafts as responses to his readings, and have the opportunity to have rich conversations.

She thought by designing lessons with multiple activities each session she would keep him engaged and happy. She also thought by using multiple books with one character they would have the opportunity to have rich conversations and increase his working or expressive vocabulary that he then could bring to his reading and writing. By using hands-on activities to respond to reading, Souta would remain engaged.

Andi's immediate focus was on vocabulary, sight-word recognition, and the use of picture clues in identifying unknown words. The differences in Japanese and English are great. The two languages do not share many common characteristics in oral or written language. Word study for Souta needed to be explicit and intense, yet, Andi wanted to keep it within the context or real books.

Words Sorts

During word sorts, students categorize words according to a common attribute identified by the teacher or the student. The type of sort is determined by what the student needs at the time (Rasinski et al., 2010). The words can come from individual word banks, writing samples, spelling inventories, and books being read to the student or by the student.

"The act of sorting, or categorizing, words into groups with common attributes is at the heart of word study practice" (Helman et al., 2012). It requires students to compare, contrast, identify commonalities, and distinguish core features of different words. While sorting, students have repeated exposure to the words and have practice with the words. They examine each word through a particular perspective each time. A word sort does not necessarily teach vocabulary unless accompanied by explicit instruction.

Open word sorts allow the student to sort the words into categories the student predetermines. A closed sort is one where the teacher determines how the words will be sorted into categories. The categories for word sorts seem endless but most common sorts include:

- Words that contain consonant blends.
- Words that contain certain long or short vowel sounds.
- Parts of speech.
- Homophones.
- Spelling patterns.
- By meaning or concepts.

Concepts sorts with pictures or objects are the least demanding in terms of English-language skills and can be a good bridge to vocabulary learning for ELLs. Picture sorts for sounds require the student to know the names of enough of the pictures to demonstrate the sound relationship being sorted.

According to Helman and colleagues (2012), word sorts need instruction that is explicit, systematic, and offers guidance to help students make connections to what they already know.

Lesson I

In order to increase Souta's vocabulary, to begin some word study, and to increase comprehension, Andi chose *The Jacket I Wear in the Snow* (Neitzel, 1994) to begin her lessons. This book is a predicable book written with rebuses and rhyme. The story is cumulative allowing the words to be repeated frequently.

Andi began the lesson by talking to Souta about the recent cold weather. They talked about the clothing they now needed to wear to stay warm. As they mentioned the clothing items they recently added to their wardrobes that matched those in the story, Andi provided Souta with a word card and picture card of the item. At the end of their conversation, Andi provided cards for items mentioned in the book that they had not talked about. The items were: scarf, jacket, boots, socks, mittens, long underwear, cap, jeans, sweater, and cap. Cap was introduced as another word for hat. Andi mixed up the word and picture cards and asked Souta to match them. Andi read the story aloud to Souta. They talked about the characters in the story, the setting, and the problem and solution. Andi had Souta fill in a graphic organizer like the one given below (figure 3.2). The top circle was used for the characters, the middle one for the setting, and the bottom one for problem and solution. Then Souta decorated the circles to look like a snowman.

Andi read the story to Souta a second time. The story begins, "This is the jacket I wear in the snow," with a picture of a jacket. On the next page, "This is the zipper that's stuck on the jacket [picture of jacket] I wear in the snow." Andi asked Souta to find the word for the picture of the jacket and to read the word on the card. She continued this way through the second reading. They chorally read through the book a third time.

Using the cloth story-telling props and a flannel board, Souta retold the story for Andi. The props provided prompts for Souta to follow.

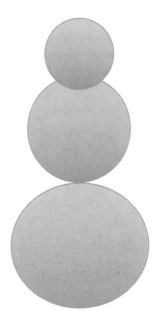

Figure 3.2 Snowman.

She used the retelling score sheet (found at the back of chapter 6) so she could track Souta's progress through the semester.

Andi and Souta went through the story in order to find rhyming words. They found me/knee, hot/lot, cries/eyes, and head/red. Souta copied all the words onto index cards and Andi would use them in a word sort in a future lesson. Using long and short vowel sounds. She decided to use –ot as the start to studying word families. Using the word family puzzles in the game closet, Souta put together all the words that ended in –ot. As a follow up, Andi and Souta constructed a word wheel using the words in the word family puzzle library for words with –ot endings.

The word wheel, pictured below (figure 3.3), is constructed by attaching a smaller circle on top of a larger circle with a clasp. The top wheel moves around, lining up the onset with the –ot rime. This can be done with any word ending. To make a word wheel for a digraph, attach two of the same sized circles together with a clasp but cut a notch out of the top wheel to expose different rimes. Print the digraph under study on the top wheel at the notch. As the bottom circle is turned, it will expose different rimes, forming different words. For example, th– next to the notch on the top wheel, and on the bottom wheel –at, –em, –ink, and so on.

Souta copied the words onto index cards and Andi kept them for future word sorts thinking she would use them for digraphs and for short vowel sounds. Andi also thought Souta might want to recreate the words with magnetic letters or with letter stamps in future lessons

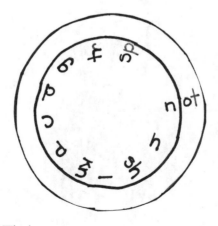

Figure 3.3   Word Wheel

as well. It should be noted that each session was a combination of word study with a focus on comprehension of the story.

Lesson 2

The Little Critter books by Mercer Mayer are part of HarperCollins I Can Read! Series. They have a strong picture to word connection, were within Souta's instructional reading ability, have a controlled vocabulary, and would be a good place for Andi to start increasing Souta's sight-word recognition. She began with the book *Snowball Soup* (Mayer, 2008). Many of the words found in *The Jacket I Wear in the Snow* (Neitzel, 1994) are repeated in *Snowball Soup* (Mayer, 2008) reinforcing vocabulary, sight-word recognition, and comprehension.

Andi began with a read aloud placing the word cards developed from the first lesson in front of Souta. She asked him to read the words on the cards and to listen for these words in the story. When he heard one of the words, he would point to the appropriate word card. Throughout the next few sessions, Andi used this text to develop a character map of Little Critter, to use highlighting tape to identify sight words, and to assist Souta to use the pictures to identify unknown words. Strategies included rereading the book chorally, employing a buddy reading of the book, and scaffolding the reading until Souta could read independently and retell the story accurately.

Souta enjoyed the Little Critter books and Andi used *This is My Town* (Mayer, 2009), *Going to the Sea Park* (Mayer, 2009), as well as others during their sessions. Souta continued to develop his character map about Little Critter. Andi continued to use the books to develop and reinforce sight words, vocabulary, and comprehension. Over several books, she identified compound words found in several of the stories such as football, lunchroom, popcorn, and so on. Sometimes she created puzzle pieces of these words for word study with Souta (see figure 3.4).

Andi used the website www.littlecritter.com to reinforce and extend the lessons with Souta. They listened to Mercer Mayer read his story *Just a Snowman* on the website. Again, Andi had Souta listen for familiar words such as boots, hat, scarf, and mittens, and identify them on word cards and recreate them using magnetic letters. She used the "read and play games" and library available at this site. Using the free coloring pages, Souta wrote his own stories for the coloring pages. He used his character map of Little Critter and his understanding of the books he had read to create his own story of

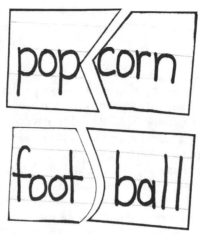

Figure 3.4   Compound Words.

Little Critter. He used that story for his readers' theatre presentation at the end of the semester.

Lessons Learned

Andi's main focus was to expand his vocabulary, increase his sight-word recognition, to use picture clues to reinforce understanding, and to retell stories with words and pictures to develop an understanding of his comprehension progress. She also conducted word study so that Souta would have strategies to identify unknown words. Souta made huge strides during his year at Literacy Space. Using the Little Critter books, above his own reading level at first, Souta would listen and retell the stories. Together, Andi and Souta would go over vocabulary, discuss how the pictures help to understand the story, and have rich conversations about Little Critter, his sister, and the events of their lives. By embedding word study, art, hands-on activities, as well as varying the reading from books to websites, Andi was able to keep Souta engaged, something she had worried about when she discovered his limited attention span. As Andi had hoped, Souta's sight-word recognition increased since he was given multiple purposes to reread text.

Andi learned how to use one book for many purposes. She started to see how word study could be embedded in the reading of one story, making the rereading one book be authentic. She saw ways to expand and integrate vocabulary lesson to lesson, build the number of words a student could identify automatically, how to build on a student's prior knowledge and interests to design and implement instruction, as well as how to use a variety to instructional techniques within one session to keep a student engaged. She began to value to use of games and manipulatives in both assessment and instruction.

Andi also had the opportunity to work with a student with beginning English-language proficiency in a one-on-one setting. She had to draw on previous course learning, her growing understanding of struggling readers and writers, conversations with classmates, and additional research in order to be effective with Souta. Her newly acquired knowledge is of great use to her in her own linguistically and culturally diverse urban classroom.

Many of the strategies that Andi used with six-year-old Souta can be used with older students with a variety of levels of English proficiency. Character maps, graphic organizers, and authentic purposes for rereading help to build comprehension, sight-word recognition, and strategies to identify unknown words. It would be of benefit to use nonfiction text as well as fiction, to find websites to extend and expand learning for the student. Using a student's interests and determining their specific strengths and areas of need should be the basis of instructional planning.

References

August, D., Snow, C., Carlo, M., Proctor, C. P., Francisco, A. R., Duursma, E., and Szuber, A. (2006). "Literacy development in elementary school second-language learners." *Topics in Language Disorders,* 26(4): 351–364.

Bear, D., Templeton, S, Helman, L. A., and Baren, T. (2003). "Orthographic development and learning to read in different languages." In G. G. Garcia (ed.), *English Learners: Reaching the Highest Level of English Literacy.* Newark, DE: International Reading Association.

Beck, I. L., McKeown, M. G., and Kucan, L. (2002). *Bringing Words to Life: Robust Vocabulary Instruction.* New York: Guilford.

Brantley, D. K. (2007). Instructional Assessment of ELLs in the K-8 Classroom. Boston, MA: Allyn & Bacon.

Bursuck, W. D. and Damer, M. (2007). Reading Instruction for Students Who Are at Risk or Have Disabilities. Boston, MA: Pearson Education, Inc.

Ganske, K., Monroe, J. K., and Strickland, D. S. (2003). "Questions teachers ask about struggling readers and writers." *The Reading Teacher,* 57(2): 118–128.

Garcia, E. E., Jensen, B. T., and Scribner, K. P. (2009). "The demographic imperative." *Educational Leadership,* 66(7): 8–13.

Gersten, R., Baker, S. K., Shanahan, T., Linan-Thompson, S., Collins, P., and Scarcella, R. (2007). *Effective Literacy and English Language Instruction for English Learners in Elementary Grades.* Washington, DC: US Department of Education.

Goldenberg, C. (2008). "Teaching English language learners: What the research does-and does not-say." *American Educator,* 32(2): 8–44.

Helman, L., Bear, D. R., Templeton, S., Invernizzi, M., and Johnston, F. (2012). *Words Their Way with English Learners: Word Study for Phonics, Vocabulary and Spelling.* 2nd ed. Boston, MA: Pearson.

Hernandez, D. J., Denton, N. A., and Macartney, S. E. (2008). "Children in immigrant families: Looking to America's future." *Social Policy Report,* 22(3): 3–11, 18–22.

Hickman, P., Pollard-Durodola, S., and Vaugh, S. (2004). "Storybook reading: Improving vocabulary and comprehension for English-language learners." *The Reading Teacher,* 57(8): 720–730.

Koskinen, P. S., Blum, I. H., Bisson, S. A., Phillips, S. M., Creamer, T. S., and Baker, T. K. (1999). "Shared reading, books, and audiotapes: Supporting diverse students in school and at home." *The Reading Teacher,* 52(5): 430–444.

Lenters, K. (2004/2005). "No half measures: Reading instruction for young second language learners." *The Reading Teacher,* 58(4): 328–336.

Lovett, M. W., DePalma, M., Frijters, J., Steiinbach, K., Temple, M., Benson, N., and Lacerenza, L. (2008). "Interventions of reading difficulties: A comparison of response to intervention by ELL and EFL struggling readers." *Journal of Learning Disabilities,* 41(4): 333–352.

Manyak, P.C. and Bauer, E. B. (2009). "English vocabulary instruction for English learners." *The Reading Teacher,* 63(2): 174–176.

National Center for Education Statistics. (2011a). *Table 3.6: State Policies Regarding Teaching of English Language Learner (ELL) Students by State: 2008–2009.* Retrieved on September 19, 2011, from http:/nces.ed.gov/pro-grams/statereform/tab3_6.asp.

National Center for Education Statistics. (2011b). *The Condition of Education 2011.* Retrieved September 19, 2011, from http:/nces.gov/fastfacts/display.asp?id=96.

National Council of Teachers of English. (2008). English Language Learners: A Policy Research Brief produced by NCTE. Urbana, IL: author

Ogle, D. and Correa-Kovtun, A. (2010). "Supporting English-language learners and struggling readers in content literacy with the 'Partner Reading and Content, Too' routine. *The Reading Teacher,* 63(7): 532–542.

Rasinski, T., Padak, N. D., and Fawcett, G. (2010). *Teaching Children Who Find Reading Difficult.* 4th ed. Boston, MA: Allyn & Bacon.

Saunders, W., Foorman, B., and Carlson, C. (2006). "Do we need a separate block of time for oral English language development in programs for English learners?" *Elementary School Journal,* 107(2): 181–198.

Tienda, M. (2008). "Fragile futures: Immigrant children and children of immigrants." *Social Policy Report*, 22(3): 16–17.

Vaughn, S., Mathes, P., Linan-Thompson, S., Cirino, P., Carlson, C., Pollard-Durodola, S., Cardenas-Hagan, E., and Francis, D. (2006). "Effectiveness of an English intervention for first-grade English language learners at risk for reading problems." *The Elementary School Journal*, 107(2): 153–180.

Verma, G., Martin-Hansen, L., and Pepper, J. B. (2008). "Using sheltered instruction to teach English language learners." *Science Scope*, 32(3): 56–59.

Vogt, M. and Shearer, B. A. (2007). *Reading Specialists and Literacy Coaches in the Real World*. 2nd ed. Boston, MA: Pearson.

Children's Literature Cited

Mayer, M. (2009). *Going to the Sea Park*. New York: HarperCollins Publishers.

———. (2009). *This is My Town*. New York: HarperCollins Publishers.

———. (2008). *Snowball Soup*. New York: HarperCollins Publishers.

———. (2004). *Just a Snowman*. New York: Harper Festival.

Neitzel, S. (1994). *The Jacket I Wear in the Snow*. New York: Greenwillow Books.

4

Amorita, a Delayed Reader

First grader Amorita was recommended to Literacy Space because she is just not on the same track as her classmates. Attending an urban public school in an overcrowded classroom, the teacher just did not have the time to investigate why there appeared to be such a mismatch between Amorita's literacy abilities and those of her classmates. When Lyle met Amorita, she was sitting with her mom outside Literacy Space. Amorita had her Game Boy in her hands playing a game based on a recent popular movie. Her mom told Lyle how optimistic she was that Amorita would improve her reading while at Literacy Space. She voiced her concerns with Lyle immediately. She was eager to share that Amorita's teacher told her she was reading below grade level, not able to keep up with her classmates, and it was of great concern to her. The mom pulled out some workbooks and Amorita's book baggie from her backpack and asked Lyle to work with her daughter using these books. Lyle had to explain that he would be using other materials in Literacy Space but he would try to integrate some of these into their work. Amorita's mom seemed anxious about this, truly worried about her daughter's reading. She said that Amorita becomes impatient after a short period of time and gives up easily.

Amorita lives at home with both her parents. She does not have any siblings and no other relatives live in the house with her family. Her mother describes her as an active and happy child. She has many school friends. Her mother stated that she is easily distracted and when reading together she often has to stop and redirect Amorita's attention back to the book.

The first few sessions that Lyle and Amorita worked together were easy going and fun. Amorita arrived each week with a big smile on her face. She listened carefully, participated in lively conversations, and enjoyed the stories read to her. Lyle was careful to plan their sessions so that he could learn about Amorita's likes, personality, attitudes about reading, and literacy abilities informally. He felt he wanted to take some time getting to know Amorita well before moving to more formal literacy assessments. He moved slowly through some interest inventories, giving them to her orally since Amorita appeared to be a more reluctant writer than a typical second grader.

As soon as Lyle started to conduct more formal literacy assessments, Amorita became moody and resistant. Lyle eased away from more formal assessments and used authentic literature matching Amorita's interests and more games to determine Amorita's strengths as a reader and writer. Using some of the games during community time in Literacy Space such as the commercially prepared charades game, Lyle quickly found that Amorita had difficulty with print and had few words in her sight vocabulary. Lyle asked her if she knew any good readers in her class and he asked Amorita what she thought they did when they came to words they did not recognize. Lyle learned that Amorita didn't know what good readers and writers do. Although Amorita had just started her second year at school and had attended regularly, she had not grasped the beginning reading concepts that most first graders own. She lacked word-attack strategies and a basic sight-word vocabulary. When asked to choose a book from the large library in Literacy Space, she chose a book she recognized her classmates reading, a book clearly too difficult for her to read independently. It became apparent that Amorita was a Delayed Reader.

Research on Delayed Readers

Delayed readers are those readers who are "late off the block." Balajthy and Lipa-Wade (2003) call them catch-on readers, those students who remain at an emergent level in spite of consistent and repeated instructional opportunities. The capacity to achieve is present but delayed readers are progressing more slowly than their classmates. There appears to be no specific learning impediment and they are not likely to be suffering from neurological deficits according to Labov (2003), yet they are not performing at grade level. They have difficulty understanding what readers do, are not aware of print activities, have little to no concepts of print, have learned few basic sight words but cannot transfer that knowledge to the learning of new words, and do not regularly participate in the literacy experiences provided for them (Balajthy and Lipa-Wade, 2003). A frequent complaint by teachers is that the child would perform correctly one day but would forget it the next day, which may be related to the teacher's failure to consider the significance of consolidated learning (Levy and Lysynchuck, 1997). Delays occur when lessons are too abstract and there is an overuse of phonemic units.

Like many struggling readers, delayed readers need explicit and direct teaching to increase student awareness of what they need to learn in meaningful contexts (Balajthy and Lipa-Wade, 2003; Gaskins, 1998). Teachers need to model and scaffold practice. "Children see and hear models of good reading; they become familiar with common written syntax and text structures; and, through choosing the books they will hear, they come to value and enjoy books and reading" (Knapp and Winsor, 1998, p. 14).

Delayed readers also need to experience motivation and success, and the materials chosen for use with delayed readers should assure them that they are successful. By assessing background knowledge, teachers can select books for which the child has prior understanding. Choosing books with familiar words and words that can be easily mapped into sounds (Levy and Lysynchuk, 1997) are more apt to assure a successful text experience. In this way, the teacher can guide the student to connect their prior knowledge, monitor for understanding, and can connect their successes with that text to what they did previously in order to succeed (Gaskins, 1998).

By meeting students where they are, instructionally, and recognizing their personal styles will help the teacher provide quality instruction (Gaskins, 1998). Observation of the delayed reader engaging in literacy practices and analyzing their writing are two effective ways to guide instruction. Yet, all this must be accomplished in an engaging and meaningful context. Delayed readers need sufficient time to accomplish literacy goals.

Some of the specific instruction suggestions for use with the delayed reader are similar to those used with emergent readers such as choral reading, guided reading, and predictable text along with lots of reading (Balajthy and Lipa-Wade, 2003; Gaskins, 1998). Not only can shared reading experiences bring out the enjoyment of reading but also can instruction in a shared reading lesson be tailored to the child. This activity models fluent reading. During the activity, the teacher can offer strategies, point out phonetic irregularities, and engage in meaningful word study (Knapp and Winsor, 1998).

Repeated readings will help build word recognition. The use of word banks and word walls will help to reinforce early sight-word recognition. Word sorts, as discussed in chapter 3, may provide experience with decoding strategies. Levy and Lysynchuk (1997) suggest that the child be familiar with the words before being asked to read them. In this way, explicit mapping between phonological and orthographic can occur. They also suggest that the child makes rapid acquisition of a reading vocabulary with word segmentation rather than whole word recognition instruction. "The beginning reader's efforts to decode a string of letters on the printed page will succeed only if the derived sound sequence is identified with a word stored in his or her mental lexicon" (Labov, 2003, p. 129).

A language experience approach may help to bridge the gap between oral and written language for the delayed reader. This could be with self-created stories or with wordless picture books (Balajthy and Lipa-Wade, 2003).

Background Tools Used with Amorita

During their second meeting, Lyle asked Amorita to pretend that she was the principal of her school and was the one who made the decisions about what kind of books the students in her school should read. He asked her to think very carefully and choose ten topics from If I Ran This School interest inventory (figure 4.1). The topics she chose were: stars and planets, dinosaurs and fossils, plants and flowers, animals and their homes, insects, reptiles, diseases and medicine, families, the United States, and holidays.

Using other interest inventories, Lyle found that Amorita likes to play games, watch television, or stay home with her parents on weekends. She likes to watch the Disney Channel, Nickelodeon, and Cartoon Network. SpongeBob is her favorite character. She likes to play with her Game Boy.

When employing a reading attitude assessment with Amorita, Lyle asked her to be completely honest but she questioned the authenticity of some of her responses. He indicated that Amorita's facial expressions never changed and nothing on the attitude assessment sparked extended conversations that occurred with other assessment tools. When asked about reading both inside and outside of school, Amorita circled all the smiley faces on the Smiley Face Reading Attitude Survey. The only indication of dissatisfaction came with reading during free time at school.

During conversations with Amorita, she confided in Lyle that she would rather have someone read the story to her than read it on her own. She said she likes to go to the classroom library and choose books that she sees the other girls in class reading. She admitted that

If I ran this school

AN INTEREST INVENTORY
developed by Deborah E. Burns and design by Del Siegle

Name _____

Grade _____   Teacher _____

If I ran the school, I would choose to learn about these ten things. I have thought about my answers very carefully and I have circled my best ideas for right now.

I am really interested in:

1. The Stars and Planets
2. Birds
3. Dinosaurs and Fossils
4. Life in the Ocean
5. Trees, Plants and Flowers
6. The Human Body
7. Monsters and Mysteries
8. Animals and Their Homes
9. Outer Space, Astronauts, and Rockets
10. The Weather
11. Electricity, Light, and Energy
12. Volcanoes and Earthquakes
13. Insects
14. Reptiles
15. Rocks and Minerals
16. Machines and Engines
17. Diseases and Medicine
18. Chemistry and Experiments

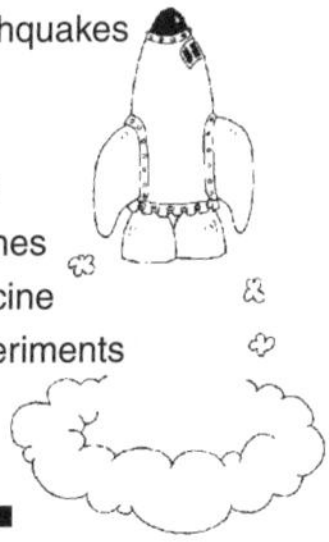

1. Families
2. The Future
3. Our Presidents
4. The United States
5. Other Countries
6. History and Long Ago Times
7. Famous Men and Women
8. Problems We Have in Our Town
9. Holidays
10. Native Americans, Asian Americans, Hispanics and African Americans
11. Explorers
12. People Who Live and Work in Our Town
13. Travel and Transportation

Figure 4.1 If I Ran This School.

Source: Developed by Deborah E. Burns & designed by Del Siegle. Permission to reproduce granted for educational purposes

she doesn't read them on her own. Although she has never been to the pubic library or a bookstore, she told Lyle that her mom brings her home books. She said she never reads books at home for pleasure and does not have any favorite authors.

Amorita brought in Chubby Cheeks, a favorite stuffed animal from her collection, as her special object to share with Lyle. Chubby Cheeks is a small, pink stuffed rabbit that Amorita received as an Easter gift one year. Lyle asked Amorita to draw a picture of Chubby Cheeks and to dictate something to her about her picture. Amorita dictated, "I love my rabbit." Lyle asked Amorita if she would like to add anything about her rabbit and Amorita said no.

Assessment Tools Used with Amorita

Lyle chose to employ some authentic assessments with Amorita. He decided that standardized assessments would cause her anxiety so decided to stay away from them. Instead, he relied on his observations of her during activities, a wordless book assessment, and find the level of phonemic awareness she owned.

Observation

Lyle was able to observe book handling behavior with Amorita during a regular read aloud. Amorita had a developed concept of print, probably from being read to regularly by her mother. She knew the cover of the book, how to proceed through the pages, that the print, not the illustrations, carried the message, where to start reading, and knowledge of a return sweep at the end of a line. It appeared that she had the concept of word and sentence but was unaware of the function of individual punctuation marks.

Lyle was then curious to know if Amorita had a concept of story since her dictation to accompany her drawing of Chubby Cheeks was not detailed. He decided to use a wordless book to determine what story language, story grammar, and story concepts she owned.

Wordless Books

Wordless picture books are picture books that tell the story entirely through illustrations with few or no words. They tell the story through carefully sequenced pictures and many contain elaborate plots, characters, and settings.

Wordless picture books provide opportunities for children to look closely, interpret, and make predictions about the story from the illustrations (Arizpe, 2011). "Because of the very nature of these texts, the reading of wordless picture books is an open-ended process in which viewers read stories by bringing their background experiences and personal histories to bear on the visual images they encounter within the text" (Crawford and Hade, 2000, p. 72). Similarly, Jalongo and her colleagues (2002) claimed, "Through wordless books, emergent readers, children with limited English proficiency, and older children with various types of reading difficulties can draw on their interpretive skills" (p. 186).

We have used wordless picture books with struggling readers as an assessment tool to discover some of their literacy strengths and needs. It offers a glimpse into their understanding of literacy-related activities as well as insights into their sense-making processes. Crawford and Hades (2000) posit that the sense-making processes used by readers of wordless books are similar to those used with text. These include the use of prior knowledge, constructing meaning, making informed hypotheses about the story line, as well as incorporating story language into the telling of the story. Children reading the wordless picture book can demonstrate their concept of story (Jalongo et al., 2002; Reese, 1996) as well as their ability to determine main ideas, make inferences based on what is happening in the story, and identify details and sequences.

By inviting children to write or dictate a story from the wordless picture book, as children generate text from the wordless book (Gitelman, 1990), they learn to write stories in complete sentences, to expand ideas to better describe the pictures, and produce meaningful stories that use linking words and proper punctuation (Reese, 1996). They build confidence as readers and writers (Jalongo et al., 2002).

Steps in Using a Wordless Picture Book

There are many wordless picture books available to use. One of the sites we found to be useful is www.readinga-z.com/book/wordless-books.php. The list is leveled and extensive. Some of the more popular wordless books include:

The Snowman (Briggs, 1978)
Hug! (Alborough, 2001)
Pancakes for Breakfast (DePaola, 1978)
Truck (Crews, 1997)
Tuesday (Wiesner, 1991).

When selecting the wordless picture book, consider the concepts contained in the book, the background knowledge required to understand the story, and key vocabulary needed to retell the story. This is especially important for choosing books to use with children who have limited English proficiency.

Introduce the book to the child. You might want to ask the child to predict what the story might be about using the title and illustrations on the cover. You might want to ask about the characters, setting, or predictions about the story line based on the cover illustration.

Begin by conducting a picture walk with the child taking in what is happening. The teacher might want to introduce vocabulary during the picture walk that would be helpful in understanding the story. Asking children if they can describe what is going on in the pictures asks for an interpretation of the illustration and invites more of a story. Asking the children "what is this?" may elicit one-word answers as children label the items they can locate in each illustration. As you and the child are going through the illustrations, ask the child who is in the story, what is happening in the story, and what the child might find interesting in the pictures.

Go through the book again and ask the child, "If this book had words, what would they be?" The teacher should act as scribe as the child dictates a story to go along with the book. Afterward, the child can reread the story with the help of the teacher, revising as necessary. For older, more able students, they can write the story themselves without the teacher having to act as scribe.

During a later session, a typed version of the story can be given to the child. Each sentence can be put on a separate strip and as the child goes through the book again, each strip can be put on the corresponding page. Again, the child can revise and change the story.

The teacher can use this experience to determine if the child has a concept of story. Does one page connect to the next throughout the text? Is there a detectable sequence to the child's story? Has the child identified details of the story from the illustrations? Has the child noted cause and effect? Determined main ideas? Drawn correct inferences? Has the child infused vocabulary introduced during the picture walk? What cultural values has the child placed in the story? Two assessment tools for using wordless picture books can be found at the back of this chapter. One is for the child's reading of the wordless picture book and the other is used to assess the dictated or written account of the story.

Using a Wordless Picture Book with Amorita
Lyle decided to use the almost wordless picture book *Good Night Gorilla* (Rathmann, 1996) since he knew that Amorita liked animals from an interest inventory previously used. Lyle began the session by asking Amorita if she had ever been to a zoo before. He asked Amorita what she had seen at the zoo, what animals were at the zoo, and what she thought might happen to a zoo at night. He introduced *Good Night Gorilla* to Amorita. He asked Amorita to make a prediction about the book using the cover. Amorita predicted that the story would be about a gorilla. Lyle and Amorita took a picture walk through the book. At each double spread, he asked Amorita what was going on in the story. He asked Amorita to identify some of the objects in the pictures and gave her the words for some of the items she did not know. He introduced words such as zookeeper, armadillo, and hyena as Lyle asked Amorita to identify the different animals in the book. He had Amorita talk about the story that was being told by pictures. He would prompt her by saying, "Let's see what the gorilla is doing," and asking what was happening to mouse.

Lyle asked Amorita to be the author of the story, to give her the words for the story since there were none. Amorita dictated the story to Lyle. Lyle used the Assessment Guide at the end of this chapter to help assess Amorita's dictated account of *Good Night Gorilla*.

From this activity, Lyle determined that Amorita had a developing concept of story even though she had been hearing stories regularly at home. She didn't use the cover illustration to talk about setting or any actions that might occur in the book. She needed a lot of prompting through the dictation. Some of her story indicated a connectedness between illustrations while other parts of the story did not. She made no personal connection to the story. The story did have a logical sequence, the words she dictated did match the illustrations, and she was able to use some of the targeted vocabulary in her story.

Phonemic Awareness

Lyle was unsure if Amorita could hear the sounds in words. He knew that phonemic awareness, the ability to aurally recognize, segment, and blend the sounds of language is important for literacy development. It is now generally accepted that phonemic awareness is a precondition for learning phonics, the ability to visually examine words.

Hallie Kay Yopp and Harry Singer developed the Yopp-Singer Test of Phonemic Segmentation that can be found on many websites to be used without cost. We found one at http://teams.lacoe.edu/reading/assessments/yopp.html. It is a list of 22 common words. The child is asked to listen to the word and then to break the word apart into its sounds. The test is not scored but the teacher can determine what the child knows about phonemes.

Lyle found that Amorita had a difficult time separating words into sounds. She seemed unaware that a word could be broken down into smaller parts. He knew that he would need to develop her phonemic awareness before implementing any intensive phonics instruction.

Word Recognition

Lastly, Lyle wanted to know if Amorita had a sight-word vocabulary. He used a commercial Informal Reading Inventory (IRI). He found that the first-grade word list was at Amorita's frustration level.

Lyle carefully analyzed the data from her observations, games played during community time, interviews, inventories, and assessments employed with Amorita.

Amorita's Literacy Profile

Amorita was unaware that there were unites of spoken language small than the word, that there are predictable relationships between the sounds of spoken language and the letters that represent them in written language. Amorita knows how to handle a book, has a developing sense of story, and enjoys hearing stories read to her. She understands the stories she hears. She is easily frustrated when trying to read books at her grade level and has limited sight-word recognition. She does not have strategies to figure out unknown words. She likes areas of science including animals and space as well as holidays and families.

Amorita's Strengths
- Has a concept of print.
- Enjoys hearing stories.
- Has a developing concept of story.
- Can dictate full sentences.
- Strong listening comprehension.
- Sight-word recognition at primer level.

Amorita's Vulnerabilities

- Beginning phonemic awareness.
- Sight-word recognition not at grade level.
- Limited knowledge of punctuation conventions.
- Needs strategies to decode unknown words.
- Develop reading comprehension strategies.

Intervention and Instructional Plans for Amorita

Lyle created five goals for her intervention plan while working with Amorita. His five goals were:

1. Increase phonemic awareness.
2. Build her sight-word recognition.
3. Develop word-family knowledge.
4. Further develop her concept of story.
5. Give her the skill to choose just right books.

To increase phonemic awareness:

- Use nursery rhymes, poetry, songs.
- Picture sorts with sound matching.
- Books with one letter as its focus.

To increase sight-word recognition:

- Sight-word bingo games.
- Books with high-frequency words.
- Keep own word wall.

To develop word-family knowledge:

- Word-family puzzles.
- Chunky foam letters.
- Stacker© game.

To develop concept of story:

- Retellings.
- Language experience approach.
- Read predictable books.

Ability to choose just right books:

- Help Amorita identify her own interests in book topics.
- Teacher her the five-finger rule.
- Give her experience choosing books from the Literacy Space library.

Lyle knew that that during his lessons, he would need to model what readers do for Amorita. He would need to use a think-aloud strategy to demonstrate his own thinking while reading and writing. He would have to carefully scaffold his lessons with Amorita. He kept reminding himself of what his professor had told him about scaffolding: I do it, she helps me do it, I help her do it, then she does it.

He would need to find predictable, that Amorita would be interested in and ones where she could experience success. Predictable books, sometimes called pattern books, have a rhyming or repetitive word pattern. The text and illustrations work together enabling the child to anticipate the words. Once children identify the pattern or repetitive phrase, the words are automatically decoded and reading becomes more fluent giving the child a sense of accomplishment and reading success. Predictable books are a bridge to independent reading. Using a predictable book would help him to incorporate word study in a more authentic way. He then thought about the word work he would need to accomplish and he wanted to do it within authentic literature. Putting together an instructional plan seemed daunting.

Each tutoring session began with Amorita writing in her journal. Together Lyle and Amorita would decide on a topic: what had occurred at home over the weekend or the previous week at school. After they talked about it, Amorita would write independently. She would then reread what she had written and would make any corrections. Through her journal, Lyle would talk about the conventions of writing, introducing various punctuation marks, upper and lower case letters, and spaces between words.

Lesson 1

In order to use authentic literature to develop phonemic awareness, begin word-family study, and story concept, Lyle devised an instructional plan using the book *The Giant Jam Sandwich* (Lord, 1987), which is written in rhyme.

Lyle showed the cover of the book to Amorita and asked her what the story might be about. He then asked her what she would need to make a giant jam sandwich. He introduced the words spade and nuisance to Amorita and told her that she would hear the words in the book.

While she was reading the book, Lyle stopped periodically to model a think-aloud strategy. He also asked Amorita to identify the problem the town was having. He asked her how the town might solve its problem.

When Lyle had finished reading the book to Amorita he asked her how the town solved its problem. He went over the predictions Amorita made at the beginning and during the reading of the book to confirm if they were correct and, if not, what had actually happened.

After reading, Amorita started to keep a word wall. Lyle had made a small poster with the letters of the alphabet listed across the poster in rows. Amorita wrote the words under the appropriate letter.

The following week Lyle reread the story to Amorita asking her the beginning, middle, and end of the story. Using manipulatives, (accompanying the book is a net, bread, etc.) Lyle asked Amorita to retell the story. He used prompts as well as the manipulatives to help her identify all the parts of the story in sequence. He introduced words such as first, then, and finally. He used the retelling assessment sheets to keep track of her progress through their work together.

In another session, Lyle asked Amorita to read along with him by pointing to the words in the story as he read. He explained that the book had a lot of rhyming words and asked if she knew what a rhyming word was and if she could give an example of one. He told Amorita to listen for the rhyming words. As Amorita or Lyle identified the rhyming words in the story, Lyle had Amorita write them on index cards. He also had Amorita identify some sight words and used highlighting tape to mark them as they read the story.

Having identified the rhymes in the book (down/town, away/hat, grew/do, etc.) Lyle typed each word individually on card stock. He attached them to the underside of an inch square tiles left over from a home improvement project and used them for a memory game with Amorita. He laid out all the tiles with the words at the bottom. During a turn, the player would turn over two tiles and say them aloud. If the player identified them as rhyming words, the player keeps the tiles and continues to play. If the words on the two tiles do not rhyme, the player turns the tiles back to their original position and the next player takes a turn. The game continues until all the tiles are taken.

In a future lesson, Lyle started a word-family study using some of the rhyming words found in the text. He began with down/town and away/hay. He left the rhyme couplet grew/do for another discussion. He used the word-family puzzles to give Amorita the opportunity to not only see the word but also manipulate them manually.

He also had Amorita recreate the words with magnetic letters that allowed her to manipulate the word families and visually recognize the patters from word to word. Amorita recorded the words in a word bank.

Lesson 2

After building Amorita's phonemic awareness, Lyle started to use predictable books around Amorita's interests. Using *Have You Seen My Cat?* (Carle, 1991) Lyle began to focus on high-frequency words to increase Amorita's automatic word recognition and would give Amorita an opportunity to experience fluency. *Have You Seen My Cat?* (1991) is written in question and answer format. The boy, in search of his lost cat, asks, "Have you seen my cat?" Shown a variety of cats such as a lion and puma, the boy responds with, "That is not my cat!"

Lyle began the session by asking Amorita if she had any pets or if she knew anyone with a pet. They talked about animals that make good pets. He introduced the book to Amorita, showing her the cover, and asking what the book might be about. Amorita responded that the boy might have lost his cat.

Lyle and Amorita read the book chorally. They discussed the various cats that the boy saw while looking for his own cat.

During the next session, Lyle and Amorita echo read the book. After reading, Lyle pointed out the punctuation marks, a question mark and an exclamation point, in the text as well as the underlined word *my* and what they meant to the oral reading of the story. He then had Amorita read the book independently. She had sentence strips of the two sentences for Amorita to read. When Amorita demonstrated that she could read them independently, Lyle cut the sentence strips apart and had Amorita put them back in the proper order.

In a subsequent lesson, Lyle had Amorita write her own book following the same pattern, " Have you seen my _____?" filling in the blank with a favorite animal. After writing and rereading, Amorita illustrated her book. Amorita used this book for her Readers' Theatre presentation at the end of the semester.

This activity allowed Amorita to experience fluency, accumulate words into her sight vocabulary, read for meaning, and use the book as a model for her own writing. She also was introduced to punctuation using authentic literature. It also allowed for a sequencing activity as Amorita retold the order of cats the boy met while looking for his own. Lyle expanded this lesson by using *If You Give a Cat a Cupcake* (Numeroff, 1991). Lyle wanted to reinforce phonemic awareness and word study during community time. He employed two games for Amorita and other students: Chip-O© and Riddle Maze©. Chip-O© is a board game utilizing picture cards that are duplicated on the game board. No reading is required. The goal of the game is to place four chips in a row horizontally, vertically, or diagonally. To place a chip on the game board, a player draws a card. The player identifies the picture, for example, fox, and can place the chip on a picture of a fox or on a picture that rhymes with fox, such as box. This constitutes a turn and the next player takes a similar turn. The strategy involved is not only to get four in a row but also to block another player from getting four in a row as well. The game reinforces phonemic awareness, as players need to listen for sounds and rhyming sounds as well.

Riddle Maze© is also a board game. The object is to move through a maze on the game board and collect cards identified as answers to riddles. For example, one clue stated, "Up in the sky each night, I usually shine so bright. Sometimes I look full and round, Circling the earth without a sound." The answer is moon so the player would want to move through a maze to collect the moon card.

Lyle also used rhyming games dependent on pictures and charades games during community time with classmates in order for Amorita to feel successful and enjoy the social aspects of literacy.

Lessons Learned

Throughout the course of two semesters, a variety of instructional practices, approaches, and methods were used to address Amorita's literacy needs. Lessons and materials were strategically chosen to address his literacy goals of building sight-word recognition, to increase phonemic awareness in order to implement explicit phonic instruction, develop a stronger concept of story, and have Amorita read books independently at her independent level with increase comprehension.

During the semester Lyle used books written in rhyme as well as poetry and picture sorts to match word sounds at the beginning, ending, and medial positions in order to develop phonemic awareness and link to phonic knowledge. He used games from Literacy Space such as Play & Learn Phonics©, games where students use pictures to identify rhyming, beginning, ending, and vowel sounds. He later used games to develop word-family knowledge requiring students to make words with tiles of onset and rimes.

Lyle used Amorita's journal to determine her level of writing ability and the progress she was making over the two semesters. Amorita went from drawing many of her first entries to writing full sentences with some conventional spelling.

Amorita now chooses books that she can read independently. She still enjoys being read to by Lyle and by her mom. Lyle suggested to her mom that they chorally read together sometimes and to have Amorita read to her from some of the books she has chosen for herself.

Lyle learned how to take a step back in order to move forward with Amorita. By determining Amorita's lack of some emergent literacy skills and strategies, Lyle needed to build a strong foundation on which future learning could securely rest. He learned to move slowly and carefully, analyzing data at each step of the process. A variety of assessments were used in a careful sequence to uncover Amorita's literacy strengthens and areas in need of instructional intervention. In order to avoid frustrating Amorita, Lyle used observation as Amorita engaged in listening, reading, and writing activities to secure data for analysis of Amorita's capabilities as well as use of assessment tools.

Using authentic literature served as entry points to develop vocabulary, reinforce and develop sight-word recognition, promote recognition of spelling patterns, and to develop decoding abilities, attention to punctuation marks, and comprehension.

All students can learn from a language experience approach, no matter what age or amount of English proficiency. The student read stories he or she has created, has ownership of the language, and helps to bridge the gap between oral and written language. Wordless picture books can serve as an entry point for students to write their own stories. They provide the story framework for many struggling readers and writers. As discussed above, they can be used for assessment and for instructional purposes.

Word sorts, reasons to reread text, and guided reading instruction will work with older populations and ELL populations successfully. Onset and rime games help to develop decoding strategies.

When working with a delayed reader of any age, instruction needs to be engaging and meaningful. The teacher must provide explicit instruction, model strategies, and carefully scaffold toward student independence. The student needs sufficient time to accomplish goals to provide a firm foundation for new learning, making sure that the student's successful performance one day will be present the following day.

References

Arizpe, E. (2011). "On wordless picture books." *Journal of Children's Literature,* 37(2): 72–73.

Balajthy, E. and Lipa-Wade, S. (2003). *Struggling Readers: Assessment and Instruction in Grades K-6.* New York: The Guilford Press.

Crawford, P. A. and Hade, D. D. (2000). "Inside the picture, outside the frame: Semiotics and the reading of picture books." *Journal of Research in Childhood Education,* 15(1): 66–80.

Gaskins, I. W. (1998). "There's more to teaching at risk and delayed readers than good reading instruction." *The Reading Teacher,* 51(7): 534–547.

Gitelman, H. F. (1990). "Using wordless picture books with disables readers." *The Reading Teacher,* 43(7): 525.

Jalongo, M. R., Dragich, D., Conrad, N. K. and Zhang, A. (2002). "Using wordless picture books to support emergent literacy." *Early Childhood Education Journal,* 29(3): 167–177.

Knapp, N. F. and Winsor, A. P. (1998). "A reading apprenticeship for delayed primary readers." *Reading Research and Instruction,* 38(1): 13–29.

Labov, W. (2003). "When ordinary children fail to read." *Reading Research Quarterly,* 38(1): 128–131.

Levy, B. A. and Lysynchuck, L. (1997). "Beginning word recognition: Benefits of training by segmentation and whole word methods." *Scientific Studies of Reading,* I(4): 359–387.

Reese, C. (1996). "Story development using wordless picture books." *The Reading Teacher,* 50(2): 172–173.

Children's Books Cited

Alborough, J. (2009). *Hug.* Somerville, MA: Candlewick Press.

Briggs, R. (1978). *The Snowman.* New York: Random House Books for Young Readers.

Carle, E. (1991). Have you seen my cat? NY: Simon and Schuster Books for Young Readers.

Crews, D. (1997). *Truck* . New York: Greenwillow Books.

DePaola, T. (1978). *Pancakes for Breakfast.* London, England: Sandpiper Books.

Lord, J. V. (1987). *The Giant Jam Sandwich*. London, England: Sandpiper Books.

Numeroff, L. (1991). *If You Give a Cat a Cupcake*. New York: HarperCollins Publishers.

Rathmann, P. (1996). *Good Night, Gorilla*. New York: G. P. Putnam and Sons.

Wiesner, D. (1997). *Tuesday*. St. Louis, MO: Turtleback Books.

Appendix 4-A   Wordless Picture Book Assessment Guide

Use the following to assess the child's reading of the wordless picture book:

	Accomplished	Developing	Beginning
The child made logical predictions			
The child could talk about what was happening in the pictures			
The child discussed the setting			
The child discussed the people in the story			
The child was able to connect the pictures throughout the book			
The child was able to make a personal connection to the text			
The child could dictate a story for the text			
The child could confirm/ reject predictions made about the book			
The child could use target vocabulary in talking about the book			

Use the student's dictated or written account to assess the following:

	Accomplished	Developing	Beginning
Story has a setting			
Story has named the characters			
Story has beginning, middle and end			
Words match the pictures			
Story has a logical sequence			
The pictures of the text are connected by the story			
Story includes targeted vocabulary			
Story includes details from the pictures			
The child revised the story upon rereading			

5

Simon, a Disengaged Reader

While the other children sat quietly with their parents or caregivers outside Literacy Space the first day, third grader Simon talked to other children and families. He was full of energy (even for any seven-year-old), had dark hair, clear brown eyes, and a smile that radiated from an impish-shaped face.

Simon found his nametag on the wall and looked to see if his tutor's nametag was there as well. Simon remembered her name was Patricia from the welcome letter he received from her the week before. When called in by Patricia, he bounded into the Literacy Space leaving his mother sitting in the alcove outside the classroom in a cloud of dust.

Simon eagerly shared a book of photographs from his summer vacation to the beach, the special object brought to share with Patricia. He described, with detail and an extensive vocabulary, the various activities he and his family participated in during their week away. "This is a picture of my whole family on the beach the first day," he said. "And this is a picture of my sister collecting shells. She has a whole bucket of them and she keeps them in her room." Patricia watched as Simon wrote captions for each photograph highlighting boogie boarding, body surfing, building sand castles, kite flying, games on the boardwalk, and so on. He occasionally asked for some help spelling some of the words and needed very little prompting to keep writing. Over the first two sessions in Literacy Space, Patricia and Simon created an illustrated memoir of his summer vacation using original photographs and Simon's narration.

When he shared his story with me, he seemed to be a careful reader, paying attention to punctuation, and self-correcting when necessary. He was excited to share and read with expression. I often was called over to listen to a story finished by one of the children, to hear a child read a selection he had just mastered with fluency, or to see the work being done by a small group of children. By becoming another audience for their work, children in Literacy Space develop a sense of pride in their accomplishments and a confidence in their abilities when given this opportunity to share.

Simon attended third grade at a local Jewish parochial school. Fluent in both English and Hebrew, Simon's first language and the primary language of the home was English. Outgoing, talkative, and expressive, our initial impression was that Simon appeared to have been sent to Literacy Space in error. Yet, reports from his teachers said he was not keeping pace with his classmates in reading and writing. Simon was underachieving in his classroom. Teachers noticed that there seemed to be a gap between his potential and the classroom performance they observed. It took Patricia quite a while to discover the concerns that Simon's teachers had for him.

When Patricia chose books and activities that matched Simon's interests and desires, all went well. In the beginning, Patricia chose books about the ocean and sea life to extend on Simon's enthusiasm about his summer vacation. She tried to use his interest to spring-board into related topics in other genres, trying poetry about sea life to begin some word study. As soon as Patricia deviated and tried to engage Simon in other genres or topics, Simon became disinterested and disengaged from the experiences. We discovered that Simon was a Disengaged Reader.

Research on Disengaged Readers

Disengaged readers are also called reluctant, resistant, and unmotivated readers. For a variety of reasons, reading serves no direct purpose for disengaged readers. Reading is not relevant to their lives and they remain disconnected from much of the reading they are required to do for school. Disengaged readers often exhibit low self-esteem and avoidance behaviors (Hettinger and Knapp, 2001). Barrington and Hendricks (1989) claimed that a disengaged reader could be indentified as early as first grade and severe disengagement over the school years was the reason many students dropped out of high school.

When there is a poor match between the student and the school setting, the student often sees school as irrelevant and disengages from the experience. The Northwestern Regional Educational Laboratory

(2000) identified disengagement as a reason for difficulty in reading and gaining information from text. Underachievement is often associated with disengagement (Demos and Forshay, 2010). This attitude often spills over to their personal, outside of school reading as well. How students perceive reading and what they understand its purpose to be has an effect on learning (Hettinger and Knapp, 2001).

Disengaged readers see reading as a chore and a source of frustration. They have trouble finding interesting books that they can read independently yet are often drawn to nonfiction. According to Hettinger and Knapp (2001), disengaged readers are often intelligent, talkative, struggling readers who ask for help inconsistently and busy teachers often discourage their book choices that appear beyond their reading level. It is in this category of struggling readers where a teacher will identify gifted students whom may be nonstrategic readers and see reading as an oral performance. Their tendency toward perfectionism causes them to doubt their ability creating low self-esteem and avoidance behaviors when it comes to reading (Demos and Forshay, 2010; Hettinger and Knapp, 2001).

Disengaged readers are each different and, often times, it can feel as though you are entering unfamiliar territory and as though we are strangers in a new land, unsure of what to do next for this particular student. It is at this point that we need to be strategic in how we come to make sense of how this student understands reading, learning, our classroom community, and more. To do this, we engage in a process of collecting information about the student (Fredricksen, 2010, p. 18).

Although this could be true of all struggling readers and readers in general, it is particularly important to read the data collected from assessment, identify the patterns and surprises, and integrate the knowledge into well crafted intervention plans. For disengaged readers, it means finding the relevance for them.

The need to engage the disengaged reader is perhaps the key to the intervention process for these youngsters. It is necessary for the teacher to identify and understand the educational conditions that foster reading engagement (Guthrie, 2004). Interest and background knowledge are two factors that help to enable students to read with engagement (Ganske et al., 2003; Guthrie, 2004). Hunsberger (2007) reminds us that connectedness between reader and text is imperative for students to become successful readers. Reading for a student's own pleasure and purpose will not only ensure more engagement with text but also the student is more likely to learn when text is self-selected (Padak and Potenza-Radis, 2010). Educators have accepted the fact that disengaged readers should be given opportunities to select what they want to read and the teacher needs to help facilitate students' choices by knowing their interests (for e.g., see Al-Hazza, 2010; Gambrell, 2011; Jenkins, 2009).

"Interest fosters persistence and a desire to understand, while topic knowledge supports children's word identification and comprehension by enabling them to draw on what they know," (Ganske et al., 2003, p. 118). What the reader brings to the text is often overlooked. Rosenblatt's (1978) seminal work on reader response theory offers the importance of what the reader brings to text in an effort to make meaning. Activating and building students' background about a topic enhances their learning (Rasinski et al., 2010). By identifying topics of interest, activating and building background knowledge with the student, teachers create an optimal learning environment in which intervention can occur. It is at this point where the student can become motivated to read.

Teachers can effectively engage the disengaged reader in several key ways. One way is for the teacher to share and model excitement about favorite books (Hettinger and Knapp, 2001) and through reading aloud to the student (Hettinger and Knapp, 2001; Jenkins, 2009) especially books that are culturally relevant to the student (Al-Hazza, 2010; Hunsberger, 2007). It means creating opportunities in which the student will succeed at a task and then building on those student successes (Jenkins, 2009; Rasinski et al., 2010).

Disengaged readers may demonstrate flat oral reading or poor fluency, as they see no need to read aloud. Fluency, the ability to read with speed, accuracy, and appropriate expression, is strongly correlated with reading comprehension (Ness, 2009). It is then imperative to provide authentic and engaging experiences for disengaged readers to work on fluency. Ness (2009) describes using joke books to help readers become more involved in oral reading and to develop appropriate intonation, inflection, and phrasing. Jokes, she argues, work in large part because of the reader's delivery of the lines. They are also short enough for focused work on the word and supports reader's development of understanding and joy in language. "Jokes may introduce new vocabulary, particularly homophones and multiple meanings of words. Joke delivery requires an understanding of word puns and word play, stress and emphasis on particular words, and the ability to approach texts in meaningful phrases or appropriate text chunks," (p. 693). Most importantly, though, working on and reading jokes to others is fun. Disengaged readers benefit from experiencing direct positive feedback about their reading.

Engaging disengaged readers requires discovering their interests and using them as entry points of comparison and catalysts for diverse readings during discussion and activities (Jenkins, 2009). Allowing students to select books, topics, and activities helps them develop a sense of ownership and will increase their motivation to read. A wide variety of books should be made available including comic books and graphic novels, computer programs, books on tape, websites to match their interests, as well as a large selection of nonfiction books.

Many disengaged readers have strong and specific interests and talents and see themselves as "expert" in that area. When teachers can identify those areas of expertise, such as a kind of video game, a sport, or even popular culture, they can work with students develop authentic ways for the students to share their expertise with others. In writing a blog about a baseball team, or creating a guide to characters in a Disney show, disengaged readers will tackle a variety of authentic reading and writing tasks.

By capitalizing on disengaged students out of school interests, teachers will be able integrate multiple literacies. Multiple literacies include digital technologies that open up the world of literacy beyond print (Kress, 2003). Disengaged readers are frequently stuck in a school-based and so limited perspective of literacy. Incorporating new technologies, Larson and Marsh (2005) argue, provide students with ways to create and find meaning in texts beyond print. Jewett (2011) provides an example as she describes the use of geocaching (www.geocaching.com) an online hide-and-seek game that utilizes GPS technology, clues, and multiple opportunities for reading and writing. Teachers can use this kind of authentic experience for both outside and inside of school experiences that build on the literacy knowledge children bring to school.

There is evidence that boys comprise a large share of struggling readers, and in particular disengaged reader (Whitmire, 2010; NAEP, 2009, 2011). While suggestions for engaging the disengaged reader are appropriate for all, we have found that some particular attention to gender differences can provide insight into methods to move disengaged boys into reading. Boys tend to develop reading abilities approximately 12–24 months later than girls. Social norms may also contribute to a perception that reading is less valued. Sadowski (2010) offers several suggestions to "hook" boys into reading. Materials with action-oriented stories and nontraditional materials, as discussed earlier, are key. It is also critical to provide links between theses materials and the more traditional academic texts. Martinez (2010) in his study of boys placed in a remedial tutoring program concurs. His students wanted to read texts with humor and action, and ones in which they could imagine themselves as characters. He also argues that while surveying classes is a good way to get to know disengaged readers likes and dislikes, the most powerful way to reach readers was through one-on-one conferences. His students valued the opportunity to build those relationships.

Students need to talk about what they are reading (Gambrell, 2011; Hettinger and Knapp, 2001; Jenkins, 2009). They need multiple ways to respond to what they are reading. For the teacher, this means being flexible and willing to adapt instruction, and individualize activities and routines to engage the student. Margolis and McCabe (2004) found that if tasks were too lengthy, difficult, or complex the student would be more resistant and less able to engage in the activity. In fact, they suggest linking new reading to prior successes and to assess carefully the amount of help offered to the student. Too much help and the learners see it as a sign that the teacher thinks they are incompetent and are less likely to engage in the tasks.

Background Tools Used with Simon

In order to learn about Simon's interests, attitudes about reading, and about his family, Patricia used the sessions creating a memoir, the If I Ran This School interest sheet, and the interest inventory found at the back of chapter 2.

Special Object

Patricia discovered a lot about Simon from the initial conversations she had with him around the photographs he brought to Literacy Space the first day of his family beach vacation. She learned that Simon came from an intact family that included his mother, father, and his younger sister. She learned that he loved all things to do with the ocean and ocean life. She learned that he was athletic since he was a swimmer, enjoyed boogie boarding, and body surfing. He enjoyed his time away with his family saying his father worked a lot and he didn't get to spend as much time with him as he would like.

When completing the If I Ran This School interest inventory, Simon had a difficult time selecting only ten things to choose from the expansive two-page list. The ten he finally selected were:

1. Life in the ocean.
2. Animals and their homes.
3. Reptiles.
4. Chemistry and experiments.
5. Math games and puzzlers.
6. Photography.
7. Scientists.
8. Sports stars.
9. Machines and engines.
10. Explorers.

In order to confirm some of Simon's interests, Patricia also used an interest inventory asking Simon to identify his leisure activities and favorite things. His favorite subject in school was science although they only had science once a week. He likes to play outside in the park on the weekends and enjoys being part of a soccer team. If he were an animal, he would want to be a cheetah because they are fast. He doesn't read magazines and does not remember ever seeing any in school or in his home. His favorite foods are pizza and pasta. He likes Jack Hannah and would want to meet him.

Simon indicated that he had a lot of interests and Patricia believed there were many entry points into any lessons she would design for him during their sessions. She already knew that the Literacy Space library had a number of books to engage his many interests; she needed to discover Simon's reading levels.

During conversations, Simon indicated that good readers read all the words correctly. He didn't like the books he had to read for school, and had trouble finding books for his book baggie from the classroom library.

Assessment Tools Used with Simon

Patricia used a variety of assessment tools to discover Simon's literacy strengths and areas that needed intervention. These included the captioned photography book he created during their first few sessions together, portions of the Fountas and Pinnell Benchmark Assessment System (2008), and word lists from an Informal Reading Inventory (IRI).

Looking over his book about his vacation, Patricia realized that Simon can spell most sight words and high frequency words correctly. His writing included details and the captions he wrote matched the pictures. He was able to focus on the one event in each photograph. He used capital letters at the start of each sentence and ended each sentence with a period. He sentence structure was simple and did not vary from caption to caption.

There was a difference in reading level when Patricia used nonfiction texts from the fiction texts supplied in the Benchmark Assessment System. It was clear that Simon brought more understanding to the nonfiction pieces. When completing a running record, Patricia found that Simon identified all the words somewhat easily. He answered literal questions fairly well but wasn't able to answer many inferential questions in the fictional pieces. However, he did show great strength in connecting to the books and commenting as he read. Simon read slowly and lacked intonation and fluency.

In using the word lists from the IRI, Simon read through the lists quickly and accurately. Yet, when reading passages of text, Simon read word for word, rather than phrasing the words for meaning. She also noticed that he confused inflected endings, words that had suffixes, and other challenging vowel patterns such as –ful, –ly, and –ious.

Simon's Literacy Profile

Patricia suspected that Simon was not a strategic reader who saw reading as identifying words but failed to see the purpose or enjoyment of reading. It appeared that the books he read for school were irrelevant for him. She realized during their various sessions together that Simon's oral language ability was sophisticated for his age. She also noticed that he had difficulty remaining on task and focused during some of the assessments. Patricia felt his independent reading was below his grade level (level L) as well as his instructional level (level M) but his listening level (level P) was much higher. It was at this point that Patricia determined that Simon was a reluctant reader. She identified the following strengths and vulnerabilities:

Simon's Strengths

- Excellent communication skills.
- Understand and uses punctuation in writing.
- Good writing ability.
- Large sight-word vocabulary.

- Strong decoding capabilities.
- Drawn to nonfiction texts.

Simon's Vulnerabilities

- Does not read for meaning.
- Does not find pleasure in reading.
- Does not self-select books.
- Is not motivated to read.
- Gets frustrated with long pieces of reading.

Intervention and Instructional Plans for Simon

Based on what she learned about Simon's interests, attitudes, and abilities the following goals were set for Simon:

Literacy Goals for Simon

1. Improve reading stamina and fluency.
2. Find meaning in reading.
3. Ability to self-select books.
4. See reading as more than an oral performance.
5. Develop ability to draw inferences from text.

To improve reading stamina and fluency:

- Use high-interest books on independent level.
- Repeated readings.
- Books on tape.

To help Simon find meaning in reading:

- Use magazines that match interests.
- Use Internet sites.
- Design ways of responding to text with physical and hands-on activities.

To help Simon self-select books:

- Teach him how to locate books with titles and topics that match his interests.
- Teach Simon the five-finger rule of find the just right book.

See reading as more than an oral performance:

- Use conversations throughout guided reading.
- Set authentic purpose to reading books of his interest.
- Use graphic organizers to aid comprehension.

Develop ability to draw inferences from text:

- Use riddles.
- Explicit modeling.
- Post-its during reading.

Patricia realized that Simon was failing to make real-life applications to his reading. Since he was such a good talker, she thought his verbal acuity was compensating for his lack of comprehension. His word-recognition skills never transferred to meaning making that was consistent that books were just not relevant for him. He believed that reading was the ability to accurately identify words at a somewhat fast pace. He lacked strategic knowledge although he appeared to be very smart.

She knew that for her lessons to be successful and to meet her instructional goals for Simon, she would have to use his interests as an entry point for all lessons. She felt if the tasks were too lengthy, he would become resistant. She thought that shorter, more varied lessons, each session would be successful. She would need to model excitement, inference making, and the relevance of texts. She also thought of hands-on activities that will keep him motivated and engaged. She also thought that Simon should be given multiple opportunities for extended conversations.

Patricia thought about Internet sites to match his interests, magazines that contained articles he might find relevant to his interests, comics or graphic novels, and a collection of nonfiction on topics about the ocean, science, and animals. She searched for opportunities for Simon to respond with hands-on activities to the books he read.

The first step was to develop a bibliography of books Simon might enjoy and allow him to select the books they would use. During this activity, she would help Simon discover how to self-select books of interest. Patricia decided to select books available in the Literacy Space library.

She went through the nonfiction library and kept his interests in mind. She also wanted to choose books at his independent and instructional levels (L and M). She chose *Dolphins* by Bokoske and Davidson, *Gorillas: Gentle Giants of the Forest* by Milton, *Science Experiments* by Webster, *S-S-snakes!* By Penner, *K is for Kick* by Herzog, and *Dolphins & Sharks: A Nonfiction Companion to "Dolphins at Daybreak"* by Osborne and Boyce. To bridge Simon's interest of nonfiction to fiction, Melisa chose *Dolphins at Daybreak* by Osborne, *Soccer Mania* by Tamar, and *Soccer Simon* by Marzollo. During the next session, Patricia introduced all the books to Simon and together they looked through them. Patricia explained how she chose the books for Simon. She had him go through the books, reading pages here and there, discussing how to choose a just right book. Simon chose *Dolphins at Daybreak* with its nonfiction companion, *Science Experiments, K is for Kick,* and *S-S-snakes!*

Lesson 1

Patricia worked at finding activities to use with the Magic Tree House books *Dolphins at Daybreak* by Osborne and *Dolphins & Sharks* by Osborne and Boyce. She consulted www.magictreehouse.com for ideas. She read through the books before meeting with Simon the next session. She secured a world map to locate the oceans mentioned in the text, Internet sources for information about ocean life and dolphins, and additional texts in Literacy Space for additional information.

Simon and Patricia worked out a schedule for reading the texts. Patricia knew that each session would need a variety of activities on the same theme in order to keep Simon's interest. One of the ideas from the Magic Tree House website was to make an underwater landscape mural. Patricia used this as an alternate to a traditional graphic organizer. As Simon read, Patricia modeled inference making and gradually Simon was able to draw inferences from the readings as well.

Each session through the books would follow a similar pattern:

- Buddy read a chapter of *Dolphins at Daybreak* and/or *Dolphins & Sharks.*
- Talk about the reading and keep a prediction log about what Simon thought might happen next.
- Compile information about animal and plant life, topographical data from the reading and add that information to the mural.
- Go to the Magic Tree House website and complete one of the games based on the reading of the books, or watch a video related to books.
- Look for additional information either on the computer or in texts.

When Patricia and Simon had finished reading the two companion books, Simon was engaged in purposeful reading. No task each week was lengthy causing him to resist. The combination of fiction and nonfiction allowed Patricia to bridge his interest of nonfiction to fiction. Simon responded with hands-on activities to his reading by creating a mural, and going to the Magic Tree House website to play games, watch videos on dolphins and sharks, complete tasks about how the environment effects ocean life, as well as going to additional websites and texts to compile more information for his mural.

Simon was so taken by the relationship between the fiction and nonfiction companion text that Patricia compiled a list of others that he might like. Because Simon chose a book about snakes, Patricia thought he might like Osborne's *A Crazy Day with Cobras* (2011) with its companion book about snakes and other reptiles.

Lesson 2

Patricia used *Gorillas: Gentle Giants of the Forest* (Milton, 1997) as the basis of the second lesson with Simon. She began by asking Simon what he knew about gorillas and had him fill in a K-W-L chart (see Table 5.1). She adapted the chart to include a column to check if what he thought he knew was correct and a place for recording where he found the information to confirm his knowledge. This often resulted in looking for additional sources when his original thinking on gorillas could not be confirmed during his initial reading.

As Simon read the book, Patricia was able to teach him the cause and effect, and the beginning of structural analysis of texts. The book

Table 5.1   Expanded K_W_L Chart

What I think I know about Gorillas	√ if you found the information to be true	What I want to learn about Gorillas	What I learned about Gorillas	Where I found the information

addresses how scientists learn about gorillas. As Simon read through the text, he was able to confirm his knowledge, answer his questions, and note other learning. He also posed new questions resulting in further research in texts and online.

Patricia also had websites to use for additional information to answer all of Simon's wonderings about gorillas. The Dian Fossey Gorilla Fund at www.gorillafund.org, The African Wildlife Foundation at www.awf.org, and the National Geographic at www.nationalgeographic.com were the websites that Patricia found to be appropriate for Simon to use.

Patricia used the world map from the lesson on dolphins to have Simon locate the places in the world where gorillas live. This led to a discussion of the rainforest and endangered habitats.

Simon had two opportunities to make puppets. Patricia found a template for a puppet at www.alphabet-action.com/gorilla_puppet.html and one for a stick puppet at www.storyplace.org. Using the information that Simon had learned about gorillas, he wrote a puppet show about gorillas to use at the Readers' Theatre presentation at the end of the semester. He enlisted a classmate to perform with him and he and his classmate practiced during community time.

Patricia also used community time for Simon to develop relationships with his classmates and to engage in reading for authentic purposes. Tapping into his love of science, Simon and a group of classmates would often play Totally Gross! The Game of Science© during community time. This game is about major science concepts in biology, chemistry, and so on, and explanations are given with each correct answer. There are question cards (for e.g., "Is the biggest cause of US forest fires: Human carelessness, lightning or fallen power lines?"), gross out cards (for e.g., "Check the person on your right for toe jam."), lab cards (for e.g., "Go to the mirror and smile. Now point to your canines."), and a jar of slime used to keep track of correct answers moved from the nostril on a picture of a face to the center for a win.

The other community-time game Simon and his classmates enjoyed was Whoonu© where players select, from cards previously dealt to them, a classmate's favorite thing. A player's dealt cards might include string cheese, making lists, the color red, snow days, and so on. All players put one card into the center face down and the classmate ranks the cards from favorite to least favorite. Players get points for picking the classmate's favorite thing.

Lessons Learned

Throughout his time at Literacy Space, Simon experienced real-life applications for reading. He was clearly touched by the plight of the gorillas. He now saw reading as more than an oral performance. He has an increased vocabulary, the ability to draw inferences, and can find meaning in reading. He still needs high-interest books to keep him motivated and on task. Engaging Simon in conversations about what he is reading or about what he has read is important for his learning. Conversations help him to make personal connections to text. Allowing Simon to be creative or providing him with alternative ways in which to respond to text gives him ownership and voice in his learning.

Patricia found that she needed to be creative in planning interventions with Simon. He was bright, articulate, and had strong opinions and interests. She employed strategies and activities that challenged him without causing him to feel defeated. She was careful in finding the correct entry points to text. In designing and implementing lessons, she felt Simon needed a voice in the decision-making process. She needed a variety of alternatives for each lesson in order to assure Simon's participation. Patricia learned how important it is to not only incorporate student interests into lessons but also give them a role in their own learning.

All teachers at all levels can learn from Patricia and Simon. In order to motivate students, teachers need to find their interests, listen to them, and find appropriate entry points when planning and implementing lessons. If Patricia had employed a one-size-fits-all remedial program to Simon, he would have closed down and he and Patricia would have not had the change to learn together.

References

Al-Hazza, T. C. (2010). "Motivating disengaged readers through multicultural children's literature." *The New England Reading Association Journal,* 45(2): 63–68.

Barrington, B. L. and Hendricks, B. (1989). "Differentiating characteristics of high school graduates, dropouts, and nongraduates." *Journal of Educational Research, 89(6): 309–319.*

Demos, E. S. and Forshay, J. D. (2010). "Engaging the disengaged reader." *The New England Reading Association Journal,* 45(2): 57–62.

Fountas, I. and Pinnell, S. U. (2008). Benchmark Assessment System. Portsmouth, NH: Heinemann.

Fredericksen, J. E. (2010). "Building conscious competence: Reading our students, sharing our practice." *The New England Reading Association Journal*, 45(2): 17–25.

Gambrell, L. B. (2011). "Ask the expert." *The Reading Teacher*, 64(6): 459.

Ganske, K., Monroe, J. K., and Strickland, D. S. (2003). "Questions teachers ask about struggling readers and writers." *The Reading Teacher*, 57(2): 118–128.

Guthrie, J. T. (2004). "Teaching for literacy engagement." *Journal of Literacy Research*, 36(1): 1–29.

Hettinger, H. R. and Knapp, M. F. (2001). "Potential, performance, and paradox: A case study of J. P., a verbally gifted, struggling reader." *Journal for the Education of the Gifted*, 24(3): 248–289.

Hunsberger, P. (2007). "Where am I?" *Reading Research Quarterly*, 42(3): 420–424.

Jenkins, S. (2009). "How to maintain school reading success: Five recommendations from a struggling male reader." *The Reading Teacher*, 63(2): 159–162.

Jewett, P. (2011). "Multiple literacies gone wild." *The Reading Teacher*, 64(5): 341–344.

Kress, G. (2003). *Literacy in the New Media Age*. New York: Routledge.

Larson, J. and Marsh, J. (2005). *Making Literacy Real: Theories and Practices for Learning and Teaching*. Thousand Oaks, CA: Sage.

Margolis, H. and McCabe, P. P. (2004). "Self-efficacy: A key to improving the motivation of struggling learners." *The Clearing House*, 77(6): 241–249.

Martinez, L. (2010). "Research for the classroom: Making connections with the boys who struggle in your classroom." *English Journal*, 100(2): 121–124.

National Assessment of Educational Progress (NAEP). (2009; 2011). Retrieved April 27, 2012 from nces.ed.gov/nationsreportcard/

Ness, M. (2009). "Laughing through rereadings: Using joke books to build fluency." *The Reading Teacher*, 62(8): 691–694.

Northwest Regional Educational Laboratory. (2000). *Motivating Reluctant Adolescent Readers*. Retrieved June 3, 2011, from http://www.adlit.org/article/27269.

Padak, N. and Potenza-Radis, C. (2010). "Motivating struggling readers: Three keys to success." *The New England Reading Association Journal*, 45(2): 1–7.

Rasinski, T. V., Padak, N. D., and Fawcett, G. (2010). *Teaching Children Who Find Reading Difficult*, 4th ed. Boston, MA: Allyn & Bacon.

Rosenblatt, L. (1978). *The Reader, the Text, and the Poem*. Carbondale, IL: Southern Illinois University Press.

Sadowski, M. (2010). "Putting the 'boy crisis' in context." *Harvard Education Letter*, 26 (July/August): 10–13.

Whitmire, R. (2010). *Why Boys Fail: Saving Our Sons from an Educational System That's Leaving Them Behind*. New York: AMACOM.

Children's Books Cited

Bokoske, S. and Davidson, M. (1993). *Dolphins*. New York: Random House Books.

Herzog, B. (2006). *K Is for Kick*. Chelsea, MI: Sleeping Bear Press.

Marzollo, J. (1987). *Soccer Simon*. New York: Random House Books.
Milton, J. (1997). *Gorillas: Gentle Giants of the Forest*. New York: Random House Books.
Osborne, M. P. (2011). *A Crazy Day with Cobras*. New York: Random House Books.
————. (1997). *Dolphins at Daybreak*. New York: Random House Books.
Osborne, M. P., Boyce, N. P. and Murdocca, S. (2003). *Dolphins and Sharks: A Nonfiction Companion to Dolphins at Daybreak* (Magic Tree House Research Guide Series). New York: Random House Books.
Penner, L. R. (1994). *S-S-snakes!* New York: Random House Books.
Webster, V. (1989). *Science Experiments*. Danbury, CT: Children's Press.

6

Cooper, a Word Caller

If ever there was a boys' boy, it had to be Cooper. His shirt was always coming out of his trousers, his hands were full of ink and marker, shoes scuffed, but he had the look of a cherub: blond, blue-eyed, just a bit chubby, and a smile to light up a room and beyond. He loved gross facts, using "bathroom" words, wrestling, and just plain running around. He knew a lot about the wrestlers of the World Wrestling Entertainment (WWE) that he watched with regularity on Friday nights. However, he was conversant about most sports. Before our sessions started each week, Cooper would have all the boys around him talking about "the game" from the previous week and it really did not matter if it was football season when he started Literacy Space, or basketball when he returned from winter break, or baseball at the end of the year. He was our resident ESPN reporter and commentator.

Cooper's second-grade teacher suggested he come to Literacy Space. She thought his oral reading was fine and he could answer many of the questions she asked the class after reading, but she could not figure out why Cooper was not "getting it" like his classmates. We had similar students from the same school attend Literacy Space over the years and, although we were hesitant to jump to any conclusions, we thought that the teacher's concerns about Cooper were a result of the school's orientation to literacy instruction.

Cooper's dad brought him to Literacy Space most weeks. He told Jennifer that Cooper learned sports and other physical activities very easily but said Cooper didn't seem to be at the same place his older brother was at the same age. He thinks that Cooper will catch up but his mother was concerned about his school performance and thought his attendance at Literacy Space would be helpful. He told Jennifer that Cooper selects books about animals most often and he reads them to Cooper before he goes to bed each night. He shares the sports page of the daily newspaper with him over breakfast most mornings.

Jennifer found it easy to engage Cooper in conversation. He dictated his responses to her about his various interests and attitudes about reading without hesitation. When she discovered that Cooper enjoyed drawing animals, Jennifer capitalized on this to select nonfiction books on strange and unusual animals, for example, fish that illuminate since they live in the dark ocean depths. Cooper always listened intently to the text and he and Jennifer were able to have interesting discussions about them when she finished reading. But when Jennifer started asking Cooper to read and discuss what he had read from some of the simpler books, their conversations were not as exciting. Jennifer did not expect Cooper to read with perfect accuracy or fluency since he was a second-grade reader but even with her assistance, Cooper was just not "getting it" from the text.

One of Cooper's favorite games to play at Literacy Space was Totally Gross! The Game of Science©. He and Jennifer would play with a few of the other children and their tutors during community share time at the end of their weekly sessions. When Jennifer read the question aloud to Cooper and the group, Cooper would usually respond quickly. However, when Cooper read the questions, his responses were sometimes incorrect and sometimes he didn't understand the question being asked. Jennifer became curious as the initial weeks went by and soon discovered that Cooper read well but did not seem to understand what he was reading. He was decoding all the words in the text, his oral fluency was strained, and he was not comprehending. He was a Word Caller.

Research on Word Callers

Word Callers are those readers who call out the words as they read without understanding their meaning. In fact, Stanovich (1983) operationalized word calling as occurring "when the words in the text are efficiently decoded into their spoken forms without comprehension of the passage taking place," (p. 372). Word Callers may have read the passage accurately but when it came time to respond to what they had read, their thinking seemed superficial, lacked text support, and they were unable to make connections to the text (Diehl, 2005). Cartwright (2010) claimed these children looked like good readers because they demonstrated age appropriate decoding skills but, in fact, had low comprehension ability. Many decode quickly and accurately but fail to read for meaning (Valencia and Buly, 2004).

The identification of word callers by teachers is not unusual since an overemphasis on oral reading accuracy without accompanying emphasis on comprehension can be found in many classrooms. Hamilton and Shinn (2003) found teachers using curriculum-based measurements in reading might overlook children with comprehension difficulties. Similarly, Applegate and her colleagues (2009) found a considerable number of teachers judged reading proficiency of a reader's speed, accuracy, and prosody, divorced from comprehension. It is important to note that these children are accurate but not fluent readers. Teachers often use accuracy and fluency interchangeably but readers need to be fluent in order to comprehend (Meisinger et al., 2010). Treating word recognition and fluency separately from comprehension leads to a great deal of confusion by both teachers and children (Applegate et al., 2009).

In classrooms where oral reading is emphasized, comprehension is often neglected. Not surprisingly, a significant number of children develop a distorted view of reading, focusing their energies on word recognition and accuracy without similar levels of comprehension (Applegate et al., 2009). Children who are word callers consistently believe that reading is about decoding (Cartwright, 2010). Word callers often misunderstand syntax, overrely on prior knowledge, and fail to integrate ideas from one portion of the text to the next (Dewitz and Dewitz, 2003).

Proficient readers must decode and comprehend simultaneously. They must identify the words on the page and construct their meaning. "It is the simultaneity of decoding and comprehension that is the essential characteristic of reading fluency," (Samuels, 2007, p. 564). Yet, for many beginning readers, the decoding demands most of their cognitive attention (Lubiner, 2004) and fail to link decoding strategies of unfamiliar words to word meanings (Katz and Carlisle, 2009) and because some words have multiple meanings, the inability to call up the right meaning interferes with their comprehension (Cartwright, 2010). The mechanics of reading need to be automatic and proficient thus freeing cognitive resources to focus on comprehension (Lubiner, 2004) or as Cartwright (2010) claimed, the student needs to be able to consider two perspectives or ideas at once. Readers need to switch back and forth or hold two ideas simultaneously in order to comprehend text. In their landmark study, LaBerge and Samuels (1974) suggested that reading is composed of two tasks: word recognition and comprehension. When readers have not developed word recognition skills, they have very little available attention to direct toward comprehension.

Katz and Carlisle (2009) remind us "students making slow progress in fluency and comprehension might need strategies that link decoding and comprehension, along with sufficient guided practice applying these strategies," (p. 325). Word callers need to know effective strategies and be accustomed to reading for meaning. They need explicit instruction, teachers modeling with think-aloud strategies with a variety of materials (Valencia and Buly, 2004). They need to learn to question while they read and monitor their comprehension. Good readers actively construct meaning while they read, taking and giving meaning to the author's words, connecting to their own lives and experiences. Diehl (2005) defined active reading as when "ideas are integrated, inferences are drawn to fill in the gaps, emotions are evoked, summaries are devised, meaning is monitored, and important points are related—all in a synchronized whole," (p. 58). This is a complex process for any reader but for word callers, the process needs to be modeled for them and explicit instruction is necessary.

For the many word callers we have worked with in Literacy Space, they believe that reading is the ability to call out the words of a text. When asked, "What do you do when you come to a word you don't know?" many will tell you their strategy is to "sound it out." Most do not understand that they should be taking meaning away from and bringing meaning to a text. So all intervention strategies need to be deliberate and focused in order to help the word caller focus on active meaning making, both at the word and passage levels. Instruction must be explicit, guided, and modeled for students. Teachers need to help the word caller slow down and focus on meaning, to have the child understand that the purpose of reading is to understand what is being read and that the rate should be flexible depending upon the reading task (Valencia and Buly, 2004).

First and foremost, books used for instructional purposes must be of the student's interest. Students must be involved in real reading situations. If we want students to make connections, to construct meaning, to ask questions while they read, and to develop a love of reading, they should be interested in what they read.

All learning involves conversation according to Routman (2000). Word Callers need opportunities to talk about what they read in small groups, literature circles, or book clubs. "Students who actively engaged in the conversation process can, over time, become reflective, critical thinkers," (Ketch, 2005, p. 8). It is through thoughtful conversation that the teacher can link decoding and comprehension instruction. By talking about what has been read, readers need to clarify their thoughts about the text and be ready to elaborate on text meaning.

Word Callers have an inability to make inferences and will overrely on prior knowledge (Dewitz and Dewitz, 2003; Katz and Carlisle, 2009). Instruction must help them make connections with the text and to integrate ideas from one portion of the text to the next. Strategy instruction to help them focus on the meaning of what they read can take on many forms. For example, the use of graphic and semantic organizers, question and answer strategies, retelling procedures, summarizing opportunities, are a few suggestions the National Reading Panel (2000) and others have suggested using when developing comprehension in readers.

Word Callers also need instruction in word recognition. In order to comprehend text, readers must not only identify the words on a page but also construct their meaning (Samuels, 2007). "Word recognition develops best when it is an integral part of meaningful and authentic reading experiences," (Rasinski et al., 2010, p. 90). In treating word recognition and fluency as separate from comprehension may confuse the student (Applegate et al., 2009). It is important to provide strategies for decoding unfamiliar words in texts and linking them to strategies to gain word meaning (Katz and Carlisle, 2009). In this way, word callers see reading as a search for meaning, even at the word level.

Background Tools Used with Cooper

It was very important for Jennifer to identify Cooper's interests if she were to engage Cooper in reading for meaning and for purpose. Just listening to Cooper in the hallway outside Literacy Space, we all knew of his interest in sports, especially pro wrestling. Jennifer decided she needed to be on the lookout for materials about the WWE and other famous wrestlers from the past and present, something she knew nothing about. She also knew that his favorite game involved science so thought she would look into the collection of nonfiction science books to see if she could find something to peak Cooper's interests.

Using some of the interest inventories, Jennifer found that Cooper liked animals, sports, space, and riding bikes with his family. Cooper also claimed liking many things including jokes, superheroes, exploring, camping, adventures, and a BIG smile around television. It appeared that Jennifer had a wide range of topics to chose from when thinking of ways to engage Cooper.

Jennifer decided to put together her own attitude survey to determine Cooper's attitudes about reading and writing. He said he liked to write because it helps him read and thought himself a good writer because he can "draw stuff." He thought that reading at home was fun, wouldn't mind getting a book as a present, but didn't like reading at school, especially completing workbook pages. Jennifer asked him if he knew a good reader and he mentioned a girl from his class. Jennifer asked him why she was a good reader and Cooper said, "Because she can read all the words without the teacher's help." He said his teacher taught him to read and when he came to a word he didn't know, he asked his teacher for help if he couldn't sound it out. His responses confirmed that Cooper was focused on oral proficiency and not on taking meaning from his reading.

Assessment Tools Used with Cooper

In order to get a better idea of what books to choose to read to Cooper, Jennifer decided to use an Informal Reading Inventory (IRI) to identify a listening level. She also decided to use a retelling procedure to determine what Cooper was comprehending from the books he was reading. Since he was having difficulty with the words in the games they were playing during community time, Jennifer decided to also assess his sight-word recognition.

Listening Level

Jennifer used the Fountas and Pinnell (2008) Benchmark Assessment System to determine Cooper's functional reading levels. She was surprised to find that his listening level was at level L, a top level for second grade. Since Cooper didn't seem to become agitated during the use of this assessment, she decided to continue to use the reading assessments, including a running record, as well. Both his instructional (level D) and independent (level C) were consistent with first grade. She noticed that Cooper did not self-correct when reading, and when he made a miscue that resulted in meaning change, he kept reading without noticing.

Jennifer was curious to know if his reading comprehension would be different if she used books that would be of interest to Cooper. She thought a retelling might give her additional information about Cooper's sight-word recognition as well as his comprehension, sense of story, and word-attack strategies through a retelling procedure. She went through the Literacy Space library level C bin to find a book that Cooper would like to use in a retelling procedure.

Retellings

Retellings have been used both for assessment and for instructional purposes. Retellings provide insights into the ways the reader, or listener, constructs meaning from texts and the ability to organize or sequence the information thereby reflecting the reader's comprehension (Gambrell et al., 1985; Moss, 2004). It involves retelling or restating the story or important elements of a passage that was heard or read (Schisler et al., 2009).

"Retelling is, by its very nature, a text-based activity that engages the reader in a personal reconstruction of the text," (Gambrell et al., 1991, p. 360). Retelling is a natural form of language behavior. We devote much of our conversation with others recounting or retelling experiences we have had, movies we have seen, conversations we have had with others, and many times books we are reading or have read. According to Benson and Cummings (2000), in order to retell a passage accurately, the reader must grasp meaning by understanding the language, apply decoding strategies, recognize the sequence of text, and infer, construct, and analyze the author's intent.

Used as an assessment tool, teachers get an understanding of the reader's grasp of information from different genres in fiction as well as expository text. The retelling can be analyzed from many perspectives: for meaning—is the retelling clear or unambiguous; for structure—is there a discernable sequence; and for conventions—spelling and punctuation in written retellings (Brown and Cambourne, 1987). The teacher should also note places in the retelling where she prompted the student to supply additional information or expand on his or her responses. When using narrative text, a teacher can assess the reader's comprehension by their ability to make a prediction, retell setting, plot, characters, identifying the problem and resolution, as well as the use of any vocabulary from the story. In assessing expository text, the teacher can assess the reader's ability to restate the main idea with supporting details, include organizational structure, use of key vocabulary, understanding of the concept(s) being read, and ability to draw inferences and conclusions from the material. Rubrics to use for assessment are included in the appendices A and B at the end of this chapter.

Retellings are an important instructional strategy. Children engaged in retellings remembered significantly more information without the benefit of explicit instruction by the teacher (Gambrell et al., 1985; Morrow, 1985; Schisler et al., 2009). Brown and Combourne (1987) found that many feature of the original text appeared in students' retellings that they term linguistic spillover. They found same phraseology, correct spelling of words never used before, and punctuation conventions appearing in the retellings. In order to retell, students devote most of their cognitive energy to construct the meaning of the passage. They reread for purpose. Some teachers have students use graphic organizers to retell as an instructional tool. Engaged in retellings over time, teachers have an opportunity to assess comprehension over genres and over time.

Retelling can take many forms. The teacher can read the passage to the student and the student can retell the passage orally to the teacher (oral to oral). This form of retelling is especially useful in determining concept of story in children whose first language is not English and also children who are at the emergent level. The teacher can read the passage to the child and have the child retell in writing or by drawing (oral to written). The child can read the passage and retell orally (written to oral). And, the child can read the passage and retell in writing or in drawing (written to written).

Cooper's Retelling

Jennifer decided to use the book *I Went Walking* by Sue Williams to use for Cooper's retelling. The book is repetitive, written in rhyme, and tells the story of a boy who meets different animals on his walk. She asked Cooper to read the story aloud and then to tell her the story as if she had never heard it before (see Figure 6.1).

From the retelling, Jennifer determined that the book, a level C text, was on Cooper's instructional level that was inconsistent to what she found when she employed the Benchmark Assessment System (Fountas and Pinnell, 2008). She thought it might be that Cooper was not accustomed to a retelling strategy but more comfortable answering

Retelling Assessment form for Fiction

Name: _____Cooper_____ Date: ___10/15_____

Genre: _fiction_____ Student Read or Listened to Text (circle one)

Title of Text: ___I Went Walking_____

Retelling was: Oral Written	4 Capable— complete and detailed	3 Developing— partial inclusion of elements, story elements there but few details	2 Beginning— Few details, essential information missing, inaccuracies or omissions	1 Not Evident Retells limited information little or no understanding, inaccuracies, omissions, confusions.
Student made a reasonable prediction, used details and/ or implied a relationship		x		
Student accurately retells beginning, middle and end of story			x	
Student gives essential details of setting		x		
Student names all characters, details about characters, and relationship between characters		x		
Student included all the events in the story			x	
Student retold the story in the correct sequence		x		
Student identified the problem in the story			x	
Student identified the resolution to the problem			x	

Figure 6.1 Cooper's Retelling Assessment Form.

questions after reading. She also noted that Cooper's oral reading was fast and he did not pay attention to punctuation. He was guessing at some words solely by looking at the initial letter in the word. He did not seem to realize when he incorrectly read a word that resulted in a change in meaning of the story or that did not make sense. When retelling the book, he had trouble remembering all the important parts of the story. He was able to give a reasonable prediction based on the title and illustration on the cover and told Jennifer that the boy on the cover was going for a walk. Jennifer decided that she would incorporate retellings into her instructional plans with Cooper as an ongoing assessment tool to help her keep track of Cooper's growing comprehension of text. She thought by using some of the books with their accompanying props, that Cooper would be engaged in thinking about his reading.

Word Recognition

Jennifer administered a word-list assessment from an IRI in order to estimate automatic word identification, estimate knowledge of letter-sound matches, and to see if there were differences when Cooper read words in isolation than those he read in context for the retelling procedure. Jennifer began with word lists below Cooper's independent level to avoid initial frustration. She gave Cooper the lists and asked her to read them and that he was not expected to know all of them. She recorded his responses on a separate sheet. She calculated the data by adding the total number of words identified correctly and dividing it by the total number of words on the list. Words on the preprimer and primer levels were at Cooper's independent level. On the first-grade level, Cooper was able to identify 80 percent of the words correctly but with delay, only 5 percent of the list was identified automatically. Interestingly, Cooper was better able to decode words in isolation than in context. She thought that Cooper could not pay attention to the two tasks of reading (word identification and reading for meaning) at the same time.

Cooper's Literacy Profile

From her assessment data that included observations, conversations, an IRI, running record, comprehension questions and retellings, Jennifer was able to synthesize her findings and put together a list of Cooper's strengths and areas in which he needed additional instruction or vulnerabilities. From Cooper's attitude survey and from the sight-word recognition that he completed, Jennifer knew that Cooper saw reading as knowing the words on the page. Although he could correctly identify words when reading, his fluency did not contain proper phrasing, intonation, or attention to punctuation that would be present had Cooper been reading for meaning. He guesses at words rather than looking for words that would make sense in text. By using books on topics of Cooper's interest, Jennifer hoped to engage Cooper in purposeful reading.

Cooper's Strengths

- Understands all concepts of print and conventions of a book.
- Has a concept of story.
- Has a strong listening level.
- Predictions are reasonable.
- Able to read independently at level B or C.

Cooper's Vulnerabilities

- Small sight-word knowledge.
- Miscues result in change of meaning.
- Guesses at words based on beginning letter when read in isolation.
- Identifies more words in isolation than in context.
- Retellings indicate that he is not grasping full understanding of story.

Intervention and Instructional Plans for Cooper

Jennifer created five immediate goals for Cooper's instruction from which she would plan lessons. These goals were:

1. Increase comprehension and ability to retell stories.
2. Develop a larger sight vocabulary.
3. Slow oral reading rate in order to read for meaning and to pay attention to various punctuation marks.
4. Develop word-attack strategies in order to solve for unknown words.
5. Incorporate more writing along with Cooper's drawings when responding to text.

To increase comprehension:

- Use graphic organizers such as story maps.
- Develop stronger awareness of text and illustration relationships.
- Retellings with flannel pieces and his own drawings.

To develop a larger sight vocabulary:

- Sight-word bingo during community time.
- Use highlighting tape to identify sight words in text.
- Encourage rereading for a variety of purposes.

To decrease reading speed and increase attention to punctuation:

- Repeated readings.
- Read along with books on tape.
- Record his reading and have him listen and read along to taped reading.

To develop word-attack strategies:

- Visit interactive literacy websites such as Starfall.com.
- Conduct word family study.
- Use word sorts.

To increase writing opportunities:

- Keep a prediction log.
- Summarize favorite parts of book and add illustrations.
- Use Cooper's drawings as prompts for writing.

Jennifer also knew that her instruction would need to be explicit and that she would need to engage Cooper in rich conversation about the books they would read together. During the initial assessments, along with informal conversations and observations during all the initial activities, Jennifer got an inkling of where to start when assessing Cooper's literacy capabilities. She used a combination of Fountas and Pinnell (2008), an IRI, and a retelling procedure. While engaged in the assessments, Jennifer also made notes of the types of reading errors he made as well as notes about his oral reading behaviors. This allowed her to design an intervention plan to meet Cooper's needs using both his interests, reading levels, and enthusiasm for reading at home. She planned lessons that would promote engagement as well as literacy learning. She was able to incorporate many his needs into the use of authentic literature, promoting comprehension and his need for reading for meaning. Cooper's competitive spirit and preference for hands-on learning allowed for word sorts, use of manipulatives, and lessons presented in game format.

The following lesson plans are samples of the activities Jennifer and Cooper engaged in during their time at Literacy Space. We encourage teachers to "spiral" lessons, to not abandon a book when it has been used but to use it repeatedly for alternate purposes. By using the same book several weeks in a row, the child has the opportunity to reread for authentic purposes, increase sight words and vocabulary, as well as fluency. The lessons below are examples of how that spiral occurred with Cooper. The same book was used over several sessions, not taking up each tutoring session, but a part of it.

Lesson I

Goals: Reading for meaning, decoding, fluency, and writing.

Text: *Peanut Butter and Jelly: A Play Rhyme* by Nadine Bernard Westcott

Jennifer began with a guided reading of the book, helping Cooper when needed, stopping to talk about the two different sounds the /ea/ made in the text. She had Cooper write spread, bread, peanuts, and eat on individual index cards to use in a word sort at a future time.

Using one of the computers, she found the song on YouTube and had Cooper listen to the song and chorally read along twice. She and Cooper went on a word hunt through the book to identify sight words. Cooper used highlighting tape to identify words throughout the text.

The second time Jennifer met with Cooper, they partner read the book together (see Figure 6.2). Jennifer suggested that Cooper write a how-to book for making peanut butter and jelly sandwiches and then illustrate the book himself. They talked about the steps involved in making the sandwich and agreed that they would skip the making of the peanut butter and jelly from scratch and use store purchased items for the how-to book. They consulted other simple how-to books to see how they were organized and how the author explained the steps to the reader.

Cooper crafted a book of his own using paper with lines on the bottom and blank on the top for illustrations. He copied some of the words straight from the book to use in his own. Jennifer noticed that many of the words Cooper included in his book were sight words he owned and were spelled correctly. Other words represented all sounds in beginning, medial, and ending positions; some were homophones. She noted this information on her Daily Record of Activities Sheet as possible word sorts in future lessons with Cooper.

In a later session, Cooper reread his own how-to book for making a peanut butter and jelly sandwich. Using it as a guide, he and a class-mate made and ate peanut butter and jelly sandwiches (no one in the class had a peanut allergy).

Figure 6.2   Cooper's How-To Book.

This group of lessons engaged Cooper in reading for meaning. He also had the opportunity to work on fluency by chorally reading with the song online. Rereading also helped to increase his sight words. Jennifer started to introduce some word study by alerting him to the two sounds they found for –ea/. She engaged Cooper in writing and tapped into his love of drawing.

In a future lesson, Jennifer will add to his collection of index cards for a word sort. She also planned to use how-to books in future lessons.

Lesson 2

A group of lessons was constructed around Cooper's preference for nonfiction books and passion for animals. The materials chosen were high-interest nonfiction books, magazines, and websites on a variety of animal topics including frogs, tigers, sharks, whales, and snakes. The texts were used as entry points to develop vocabulary, reinforce and increase sight words, promote recognition of spelling patterns, and develop coding abilities.

Cooper worked on creating an animal trivia game. Jennifer identified a number of books in Literacy Space for Cooper to read. She also used articles in *Time for Kids Magazine, National Geographic Kids Magazine,* and *Ranger Rick.* She collected a number of articles about frogs.

Jennifer and Cooper engaged in partner reading of one of the articles. She began by previewing the magazine by looking at picture of the various types of frogs. They compared the various frogs' appearances. They began with a partner read and then shared what they had learned about frogs. Cooper drew his favorite frog in a blank book and then labeled parts of the frog using what he had learned about frogs. He then used the facts about frogs to create riddle for his animal guessing game.

Jennifer focused Cooper's attention on the consonant blend /fr/. She had Cooper sort various pictures with the /fr/ consonant blend.

Jennifer then introduced the book *Sharks* (Berger and Berger, 2003) to Cooper. She introduced the /sh/ consonant digraph to him and told him to watch for the sound in the beginning, middle, and end of the words and gave him the following examples: fish, bushes, shop. She had Cooper sort through picture cards of object having the /sh/ consonant diagraph.

They partner read *Sharks* and Cooper paid attention to words containing /sh/. Again, Cooper used his blank book to draw a picture of his favorite shark, made notes on sharks, and created a riddle for his guessing game.

Jennifer also used the following websites for Cooper to learn about animals: http://animal.discovery.com has games, videos, and information about many different animals; www.bagheera.com has information about endangered animals, and www.nwf.org has a children's section. She also located sites for specific animals.

Using these, Cooper created more riddles for his animal guessing game. Jennifer also collected words using different consonant digraphs for word study and word sorts.

Toward the end of the semester, Jennifer located sample game boards by conducting a Google search. Cooper went through his notes and created many animal trivia cards for his game using the interesting facts he had found in books, magazines, and online. Some examples include:

I live in the rainforest in Central America. I love to eat insects. I live near water. What am I?

I have been around for 400 million years. I have the most powerful jaw on the planet. I love to eat seals and dolphins. What am I?

I have a head like a horse, a tail like a monkey, a snout like an aardvark, and eyes   like a lizard. I can come in many colors. What am I?

Cooper used his riddles for his Readers' Theatre presentation at the end of the semester. He used the riddle cards from his game and asked the audience to give the answers. He was confident and enjoyed having a crowd to hear his riddles.

Lessons Learned

Cooper was a struggling second-grade reader who was not reading for meaning. He thought good readers identified all the words on a page. He read quickly, using initial letters of words to guess at whole words, neglected punctuation, context clues, word-attack strategies, and picture clues to derive meaning from text. He had a small sight.

During Cooper's two semesters at Literacy Space, he was given the opportunity to read orally almost each session allowing him to slow his reading pace, pay attention to punctuation, and to look for meaning in all text. He now has word-attack strategies to help him determine words that are not immediately recognizable. To target Cooper's literacy goals, lessons were deliberately designed around his interests of animals and sports. Therefore, materials chosen included high-interest nonfiction books and magazines on a variety of animal and sports topics. The texts were used as entry points to develop vocabulary and decoding abilities, reinforce and build sight words, and most importantly, to increase his comprehension.

Overall, Cooper demonstrated a stronger appreciation and understanding of the books he read. His writing skills were stronger as his words were more reflective of his thoughts.

Jennifer learned which assessments may work best for each or all students and how to use them to drive instruction further within a whole or small group, as well as with one-on-one tutoring. She realized that administering a variety of inventories was worth the time they took because it allowed her to individualize instruction to meet Cooper's instructional needs. However, the most important change in her practice that she experienced as a result of her time in Literacy Space was the confidence she gained as a literacy educator. She realized that she did have the knowledge and experience to find a student's strengths and difficulties. She also gained confidence in methodologies she used and learned how easily she could adapt them for specific needs.

Many of the lessons Jennifer used with Cooper can be adapted for use with other populations of students rather than just with word callers. The retelling procedure has been used with English Language Learners (ELLs) as well as with older struggling readers. It can be used with fiction as well as nonfiction text. Since teachers have the option of reading the text aloud to students, the procedure of having the students read orally or silently and then deciding if the students should retell orally or in writing (ELLs may prefer to draw first) can be adapted to large populations of students as both as an assessment and as an instructional strategy.

Strategies that have been suggested for older word callers have been conversations with the author, literature discussion groups, as well as reciprocal teaching. These strategies are of use with older struggling readers who have been identified as having trouble reading for meaning. Teachers might also teach the strategy of summarizing after reading to help the word caller identify the important parts of the text, to help them focus on what they have learned from the reading, and help to connect the important ideas to each other. Cloze procedures can be used to help the student use context clues to identify unknown vocabulary, again requiring the student find meaning in text. In each of these instructional strategies, the students need to engage in rereading allowing for increase in comprehension, vocabulary, and sight-word recognition.

References

Applegate, M. D., Applegate, A. J., and Modla, V. B. (2009). " 'She's my best reader; she just can't comprehend': Studying the relationship between fluency and comprehension." *The Reading Teacher,* 62(6): 512–521.

Benson, V. and Cummins, C. (2000). *The Power of Retellings: Developmental Steps for Building Comprehension.* Bothell, WA: WrightGroup/McGraw-Hill.

Brown, H. and Cambourne, B. (1987). *Read and Retell.* Portsmouth, NH: Heinemann.

Cartwright, K. B. (2010). *Word Callers.* Portsmouth, NH: Heinemann.

Dewitz, P. and Dewitz, P. K. (2003). "They can read the words but they can't understand: Redefining comprehension assessment." *The Reading Teacher,* 56(5): 422–435.

Diehl, H. L. (2005). "Snapshots of our journey to thoughtful literacy." *The Reading Teacher,* 59(1): 56–69.

Fountas, I. and Pinnell, S U. (2008). *Benchmark Assessment System.* Portsmouth, NH: Heinemann.

Gambrell, L. B., Koskinen, P. S., and Kapinus, B. A. (1991). "Retelling and the reading comprehension of proficient and less proficient readers." *Journal of Educational Research,* 84(6): 356–362.

Gambrell, L. B., Pfeiffer, W., and Wilson, R. (1985). "The effects of retelling upon comprehension and recall of text information." *Journal of Educational Research,* 78(4): 216–220.

Hamilton, C. and Shinn, M. R. (2003). "Characteristics of word callers: An investigation of the accuracy of teachers' judgments of reading comprehension and oral reading skills." *School Psychology Review,* 32(2): 228–240.

Katz, L. A. and Carlisle, J. F. (2009). "Teaching students with reading difficulties to be close readers: A feasibility study." *Language, Speech, and Hearing Services in Schools,* 40(3): 325–340.

Ketch, A. (2005). "Conversation: The comprehension connection." *The Reading Teacher,* 59(1): 8–13.

LaBerge, D. and Samuels, S. J. (1974). "Toward a theory of automatic information processing in reading." *Cognitive Psychology,* 6(2): 293–323.

Lubiner, S. (2004). "Help for struggling upper grade elementary readers." *The Reading Teacher,* 57(5): 430–438.

Meisinger, E. B., Bradley, B. A., Schwanenflugel, P. J., and Kuhn, M. R. (2010). "Teachers' perceptions of word callers and related literacy concepts." *School Psychology Review,* 39(1): 54–68.

Morrow, L. M. (1985). "Retelling stories: A strategy for improving young children's comprehension, concept of story structure, and oral language complexity." *The Elementary School Journal,* 85(5): 646–661.

Moss, B. (2004). "Teaching expository text structures through information trade book retellings." *The Reading Teacher,* 57(8): 710–718.

National Institute of Child Health and Human Development. (2000). *Report of the National Reading Panel. Teaching Children to Read: An Evidence Based Assessment of the Scientific Research Literature on Reading and Its Implications for Reading Instruction: Reports of the Subgroups* (NIH Publication No. 00-4754). Washington DC: US Government Printing Office.

Rasinski, T. V., Padak, N. D., and Gawcett, G. (2010). *Teaching Children Who Find Reading Difficult,* 4th ed. Boston, MA: Allyn & Bacon.

Routman, R. (2000). *Conversations: Strategies for Teaching, Learning, and Evaluations.* Portsmouth, NH: Heinemann.

Samuels, S. J. (2007). "The DIBELS test: Is speed of barking at print what we mean by reading fluency?" *The Reading Research Quarterly,* 42(4): 563–566.

Schisler, R., Joseph, L. M., Konrad, M., and Alber-Morgan, S. (2009). "Comparison of the effectiveness and efficiency of oral and written retellings and passage review as strategies for comprehending text." *Psychology in the Schools,* 47(2): 135–152.

Stanovich, K. E. (1983). "Matthew effects in reading: Some consequences of individual differences in the acquisition of literacy." *Reading Research Quarterly,* 21(4): 360–407.
Valencia, S. W. and Buly, M. R. (2004). "Behind test scores: What struggling readers really need." *The Reading Teacher,* 57(6): 520–531.

Children's Literature Cited

Sloan, P. and Sloan, S. (1994). *What If...?* Marlborough, MA: Sundance/ Newbridge Publishing
Westcott, N. B. (1992). *Peanut Butter and Jelly: A Play Rhyme.* London, England: Puffin
Williams, S. (1996). *I Went Walking.* Boston, MA: Houghton Mifflin Harcourt Books.

Appendix 6-A   Retelling Assessment Form
for Fiction

Name:_____ Date: _____

Genre:_____ Student Read or Listened to Text (circle one)

Title of Text:_____

Retelling was: Oral Written	4 Capable: Complete and detailed	3 Developing: Partial inclusion of elements, story elements, but few details	2 Beginning: Few details, essential information missing, inaccuracies, or omissions	1 Not Evident: Retells limited information little or no understanding, inaccuracies, omissions, confusions.
Student made a reasonable prediction, used details and/or implied a relationship				
Student accurately retells beginning, middle and end of story				
Student gives essential details of setting				
Student names all characters, details about characters, and relationship between characters				
Student included all the events in the story				

Student retold the story in the correct sequence				
Student identified the problem in the story				
Student identified the resolution to the problem				

Indicate the vocabulary the student included in the retelling from the story.

_____

_____

_____

Indicate the places where the student was prompted to expand on response.

_____

_____

_____

Scoring:

26–32	Independent Level
18–25	Instructional Level
10–17	Frustration Level
0–9	Inappropriate

Appendix 6-B   Retelling Assessment Form for Expository Text

Name:_____ Date: _____

Genre:_____ Student Read or Listened to Text (circle one)

Title of Text:_____

Retelling was: Oral Written	4 Capable: Complete and detailed	3 Developing: Partial inclusion of elements	2 Beginning: Few details, essential information missing, inaccuracies, or omissions	1 Not Evident: Retells limited information little or no understanding, inaccuracies, omissions, confusions.
Student retells important concepts from text				
Student includes supporting details				
Student uses organizational structure in retelling				
Student uses key vocabulary in retelling				
Student demonstrates understanding of concepts using textual evidence				

Indicate the vocabulary the student included in the retelling from the text.

_____

_____

_____

Indicate the places where the student was prompted to expand on response.

_____

_____

_____

Scoring:

17–20	Independent Level
12–16	Instructional Level
7–11	Frustration Level
0–6	Inappropriate

7

Emma, a Student with Possible Learning Disabilities

Emma, a slight, shy, third grader from a local public school, traveled to Literacy Space with several other children from her school. While her peers boisterously meandered through the hallways and initiated games and conversations with the other children waiting for tutoring, Emma always held back. She appeared to be both part of and separate from the group.

During the initial tutoring sessions, Emma always responded to her tutor Janice's questions, but frequently with a single word answer. Even when discussing her special object, a well-loved stuffed cat Mittens, Emma was reticent. Emma's tutor was puzzled by Emma's single word answers to her questions about where Mittens came from and what she liked to do with Mittens. Emma didn't appear difficult or angry or resistant, behaviors Janice had experienced with other struggling readers. Janice realized that Emma was unique and that it was her responsibility to learn more.

Emma's mother shared with Janice a school report card. While her teacher noted Emma's sweet disposition and good behavior, Emma's inconsistent performance in reading was noted. The teacher wrote that while Emma worked very hard, her scores on the school's standardized reading assessments were below grade level. Reading, the teacher noted, didn't seem to "stick" with Emma. She was receiving small-group instruction as part of her schools Response to Intervention (RTI) plan but there too, Emma's performance was very inconsistent. The school had recommended extra tutoring for Emma and referred her to Literacy Space. If Emma's reading performance didn't improve, the school was considering having her repeat third grade and referred for an evaluation for special education services. Emma's mom, a single parent with two older children, was concerned. Would the tutoring at Literacy Space help? Why was reading so difficult for Emma? Did Emma need to be evaluated? Did she have a learning disability?

Research on Learning Disabilities

The term "learning disability" is complex and has been marked by controversy (Connor, 2012). This label or diagnosis doesn't have a specific physical indicator as a disability such as blindness. As such, it is considered "soft" and so open to changing definitions (Gersten et al, 2001). Thus, a brief summary of the historical context of the designation is useful to set the context.

The term "learning disability" was introduced in the early 1960s to describe children who experienced delays in speech, reading and writing, math or another school-based subject not due to mental retardation, social or educational deprivation, or severe emotional or physical issues (Hallahan and Mercer, n.d.). By the 1970s, Congress passed Public Law 94–142, the Education for All Handicapped Children Act. This established learning disabilities as a category for funding of services for identified children. A central finding for the definition, for this act, was a significant discrepancy between intellectual ability, determined through IQ testing and a student's achievement, measured by standardized test scores. One consequence of this method of classification of students was that there was, in the 1970s through the 1990s, a significant increase in students labeled as learning-disabled (LD) (Hallahan and Mercer, n.d.). Researchers and educators grew concerned and four criticisms of this model emerged (Mesmer and Mesmer, 2008). First, the model relied on significant discrepancy between IQ and achievement that in practice meant that the student needed to fail before support could be offered. Second, educators believed that finding a discrepancy was not needed as struggling learners benefitted from the same instructional strategies. Third, focus on discrepancy redirects attention from moving forward with the learner. Finally, the discrepancy model has, as noted above, increased, inaccurately, the numbers of students labeled as LD, which may be limiting educational options for them.

In an effort to address the needs of struggling students, in 2004, Individuals with Disabilities Education Act (IDEA)Public Law k108–446 introduced RTI. In place of the discrepancy model, this law states that identifying learning disabilities should be based on a student's response to multitiered instructional interventions (Federal Register, 2006). This process would begin in the general education classroom, with research supported whole class instruction, Tier 1. For students who were assessed as struggling, more focused interventions, such as targeted weekly or daily small-group instruction, are given, Tier 2. If students continue to need more support, Tier 3 or individualized tutoring and referral to more extensive diagnostic assessment is warranted. Accordingly, students who respond more quickly to the designated interventions are deemed less likely to have a learning disability than students who make slower or limited progress. A learning disability should not be diagnosed because of inappropriate instruction, socioeconomic status, culture, emotional issues, sensory issues, or English as a Second Language (Mesmer and Mesmer, 2008).

This approach toward referral of students to special education only after successive work with different instructional formats now includes more general education teachers in the process. Previously, too many students who struggled with reading were inappropriately referred to special education. Demos and Forshay (2010) state

> Diverse learners are more likely to be referred for additional testing and placement in special education programs because achievement tests typically do not access literacy skills that they may have acquired outside school and these skills often differ from the ones children are expected to have when they enter school. (p.57)

Ideally, then the RTI process is designed to support students who are struggling as soon those struggles become apparent, rather than waiting for a failure. Mesmer and Mesmer (2008) state

> RTI is a process that incorporates both assessment and intervention so that immediate benefits come to the student. Assessment data are used to inform interventions and determine the effectiveness of them. As a result of the intervention-focused nature of RTI, eligibility services shift toward a supportive rather than a sorting function. (p. 287).

When working, this model would decrease the referrals to special education where, in some instances, the instructional model still doesn't meet the needs of the students.

Hughes and Dexter (2011) report on the typical components of RTI and the beginnings of the research base on effective implementation of RTI. The primary components of RTI are "scientifically based core curriculum, universal screening, progress monitoring, and decisions about adequate progress in subsequent tiers." (p. 5). Five components of effective early reading—phonemic awareness, phonics, fluency, vocabulary, and text comprehension—are regarded as the key elements for reading by the National Reading Panel (NRP, 2000). Universal screening is a collection of classroom-based assessments, typically administered three times a year, of the relevant target reading areas. While there is agreement as to many of the screening measures, it's important to note that there is no consensus as to what criteria to be used to identify students who are at risk in Tier 1. While this enables some flexibility for states and districts, it also makes it difficult to compare programs and effectiveness.

Progress monitoring in RTI is the process by which teachers and other school-based educators assess and analyze data about students' reading behaviors. According to Hughes and Dexter (2011), it is recommended that assessment after 8–10 weeks is appropriate to gauge the impact of the intervention. The goal of careful progress monitoring is to carefully target and plan assessment based upon the assessment, documentation of student progress, clearer and potentially higher expectations for students, and more information for communication within the team and for families. According to Hughes and Dexter, curriculum-based monitoring, that is classroom-based assessments that target curriculum taught, are the most research supported instruments for progress monitoring.

There is less agreement about the criteria for making decisions about moving student from Tier 2 to Tier 3, which in many instances is referral to special education services. "There is no clear methodological definition of how or when a student should be identified as a nonresponder to intervention. This lack of clarity poses a problem for RTI as an identification tool because of the potential for inconsistent identification of LD (e.g., under 2%, over 7%)," (p. 8).

How is RTI working? According to Hughes and Dexter (2011) who reviewed 13 published studies, all reported some academic improvement for students. In the main, studies reported on the impact of RTI on early reading and math skills and so RTI's impact on other curricula areas and for older students is yet to be seen. Finally, there was little evidence, as yet, that RTI resulted in reduced rates of special education referrals and placements.

Response to Intervention and the Classroom Teacher

As RTI is relatively new, and the model begins with classroom-based assessment and intervention, it is relevant to look at how RTI particularly impacts classroom teachers of reading.

In an article in *The Reading Teacher*, Johnston (2010) distinguishes between looking at RTI as an identification process, as discussed above, which focuses on the strengths and needs of students and an instructional framework, focused on the kind and quality of teaching, which has a direct relationship to the goals of literacy teachers. He presents a critical perspective in understanding our roles, as literacy teachers and educators. He argues that teacher expertise in literacy assessment, curriculum planning, and instructions, and in collaboration with other school educators are key in supporting struggling readers. Researcher who studied teachers with increased training in literacy instruction and interventions found that the children taught by these teachers made significant improvement (Al Otaiba and Torgesen, 2007; Dorn and Schubert, 2008)

In a similar vein, Lose (2007) discusses four fundamental principles of quality and successful approach to RTI, which resonate with our approach at Literacy Space. First, she argues that any RTI program needs to focus on the child, not a group. While instruction, in the first two tiers may take place in whole classrooms or in small groups, careful, responsive attention to the particular literacy-learning path each struggling reader takes. Second, a valid RTI approach can only be measured in the successful response or learning of each child; "The intervention must be appropriately intensive, delivered without delay and tailored precisely to the individual child." (p. 277). Third, Lose asserts that it is the skilled teachers, not the programs, that teach children to read, and it is imperative to have a skilled, knowledgeable teacher who is able to make critical teaching decisions to support a child's literacy learning. One-size-fits-all programs, she argues, may make problems worse. Finally, Lose advocates for continued and high-quality professional development for teachers. Working with struggling readers is challenging, even for experienced teachers. Because of these demands, it is important that teachers have sustained access to professional development in literacy education to develop their expertise.

Diagnosis of Learning Disabilities

In 2011, the National Joint Committee on Learning Disabilities (NJCLD, 2011) released a report strongly advocating "comprehensive assessment and evaluation of students with learning disabilities by a multidisciplinary team for the identification and diagnosis of students with learning disabilities" (p. 3). It was critical, the report stated, that the assessment process be conducted by a team of professionals with expertise in their areas, multiple and valid instruments used, and that the assessments incorporate both formal and informal data. The goal of this kind of assessment is to "identify the specific areas of strength and unique educational needs" of students (p. 10). It further argues that learning disabilities "may be manifested differently among individuals over time, in severity, and across settings. Furthermore, the manifestations of learning disabilities are often subtle and may be hidden when students use compensatory or avoidance strategies" (p. 10). Currently, children who continue to experience difficulties in reading, despite interventions, small group and individual, will then be assessed by a team of professionals, including special educators, school psychologist, and occupational and speech therapist.

Characteristics of Readers with Learning Disabilities

What is the difference between a struggling reader, as we've discussed in the earlier chapters, and one who has a learning disability? One distinction, according to Fuchs and Fuchs (2006) is the severity. According to their analysis of research on learning disabilities and readers, children with learning disabilities have more severe problems learning to read than poor readers.

Some of the signs of learning disabilities include sustained difficulty in early reading activities such as trouble learning the alphabet, rhyming, or making connections from letters to sounds. Other signs in older children might be difficulty with writing, spelling, and handwriting. Often signs of learning disabilities include problems with understanding jokes, following directions, and trouble organizing thought and carrying on a conversation. (NICHCY, 2004).

A commonly recognized learning disability impacting learning to read is dyslexia. Dyslexia, as it is now understood, has neurological roots, is language-based, and characterized by difficulties in word recognition and poor spelling and decoding skills (Individuals with Disabilities Act, IDA, 2007). While some of these issues are similar to those of younger struggling readers, dyslexic readers do not outgrow these issues (Washburn, Joshi, and Cantrell, 2011). Instead, children who are accurately assessed and provided targeted, structured instruction are able to make progress.

Historically, LD students were believed to have some kind of deficiency in their cognitive processing that resulted in difficulties in learning. More recent research in learning disability argues that LD students are inefficient in the ways they process information. Gersten et al. (2001) asserts, "...while students with learning disabilities possess the necessary cognitive tools to effectively process information, for some reason they do so very inefficiently. Most researchers suspect that the breaks occur in the domain of strategic processing and metacognition," (p. 280). Proficient readers are able to call upon multiple strategies to support their understanding as they read a variety of texts. Without an efficient way to do that, LD readers struggle or abandon the reading.

Another challenge for LD children is understanding and using the support of text structures. Narrative or storybooks have predicable structures that proficient readers have developed with little explicit instruction. LD readers do not have this strong sense of how stories are "supposed to be" and so process each text anew without the benefits of understanding the story structure. This is even more profound in reading expository texts where there is even greater variation in text structure. Difficulty with understanding and using the text structure makes literal and inferential comprehension hard.

Moving to the word level, children with learning disabilities may also struggle with vocabulary. Some are challenged by abstract language. This impacts reading in more academic contexts and in being able to move from concrete understanding to the more conceptual.

Bloom and Taub (2003) summarize some of the signs that suggest a specific language-based disability. They include:

• Learning to talk late.
• Poor handwriting.

- Weak written work but strong oral participation.
- Spelling better than reading or reading better than spelling.
- Difficulty in reading comprehension.
- Avoidance of reading but interested in information.
- Strong ability in drawing.
- Emotional responses.
- Family history.
- Variety in performance.

Effective Strategies for Learners with Suspected Learning Disabilities

Students with reading disabilities are all different and benefit most from carefully tailored interventions. Yet, research in effective practices provide insights into how to best support these learners in general education settings.

For some students with reading disabilities, a focus on the phonemic awareness and decoding is the essential first step. These students have experienced difficulty in making the connections between the sounds of language and the visual symbols. There are many programs and trainings for teachers to teach students who have not been able to learn through whole class instruction. For example, Bloom and Taub (2003) present a highly structured and sequenced intervention program that introduces students to letters and sounds, one by one. Their sequence is organized by "auditory, visual, and kinesthetic factors, rather than by alphabetical order," (p. 16). The lessons in their program include reviews of previously learned sound or sounds, activities with letter flash cards, introduction of a new sound, dictation, decodable text reading, and word games. This and other commercial programs, such as Wilson Reading System, are based on the Orton-Gillingham approach to reading remediation. The hallmarks of this approach are multisensory activities, explicit, structured, and sequenced lessons about sounds and letters, and personalized assessment and instruction.

In one case study, Morris and Gaffney (2011) describe the reading intervention with a 12-year-old boy, Luke, who, at fifth grade read at a first-grade level. Initially, Luke was placed in an intensive phonics program, which increased his decoding skills. Still, his overall progress was slow. He attended a university-based tutoring program, which focused on increasing his fluency with attention to the relationship to comprehension. The intervention was designed to draw upon his strong interest in social studies and history, and build daily fluency activities into his reading. The intervention also was constructed to use materials at his instructional level. Additionally, this intervention provided Luke with targeted and continuous feedback on his performance. Luke made exceptional progress in his reading through a focused intervention that supported his oral reading fluency.

Similarly, Osborn et al. (2007) analyzed the impact of tutoring on LD children. The intervention was intensive (3–4 days per week) and included guided reading, focused instruction on spelling and vocabulary, and time for work on specific skills. Comparing pre- and posttest scores on a matched group who received the intervention and those who didn't, the researchers found that children who received this intensive tutoring outperformed those who didn't on measures of reading comprehension, fluency, and skills. The authors argue that a coherent and balanced intervention program can successfully meet the needs of reading disabled children in a school setting.

Hollenbeck (2010) demonstrated the importance of providing students with learning disabilities explicit guidance in making connections to making meaning as they read. Explicit instruction includes extensive teacher modeling, structured and guided practice, teacher feedback to students on their performance, and the carefully planned withdrawal of teacher support so that students can achieve independence. She advised, "It is important to consistently link a new strategy back to the personal reading experiences of students with LD so they grow familiar with the idea of applying strategies while reading...It is also important for students with LD to know that comprehension strategies can be applied at different times (i.e., before reading, during reading, and after reading). Students with LD should be explicitly taught that questions have different purposes depending on when they are asked." (p. 218).

To close, Connor (2011) offers several wise suggestions that resonate with our view of seeing children first and moving beyond educational labels (Jensen, Tuten, Hu and Eldridge, 2010). He explains the perspective of Disability Studies in Education (DSE) that, recognizing the limits of a deficit model of special education and disability, reorients disability as normal, a different normal. This view embraces the diversity of disability and of all children. In planning instruction for children, he suggests creating multiple access points in lessons to support students' ability to use what they know as a start to new concepts or skills, carefully observing and listening to students, and being flexible and creative. It is important, he urges for teachers to understand that students who struggle have good and bad days and so to not take personally the frustrations and sometimes anger of those students. It is important for teachers to know and use appropriately accommodations (changes made that enable student to participate by bypassing a weakness) or an intervention (targeted activities to build up area of weaknesses) in working with individual children.

Background Tools Used with Emma

From the outset, Emma's mother, Louise, was very anxious and emotional in talking about Emma's problems in school. Through the parent interview, Janice discovered that Louise had concerns about Emma from early childhood. She probed further about developmental milestones in language development to see what clues about Emma's strengths and struggles she could learn. Louise reported that Emma began speaking late—at about 30 months. This was of concern to Louise, since she had two brothers who had learning issues in school. In preschool and kindergarten teachers noted Emma's perceptive comments and interesting stories, and didn't indicate any concern about her literacy development. Yet, Louise remained concerned and shared with Janice that when she participated in family reading days and other school activities during kindergarten she observed other children reading and writing in more advanced ways than Emma. When Louise brought up her concerns to the teachers and principal in Emma's school, she was told that Emma was a lovely, well-behaved girl and to give her some more time. Because the reading program at Emma's school was highly structured and Emma was adept at following along with her peers, she did not stand out having a particular learning issue. In third grade, however, the reading demands began to grow and Emma was increasingly more upset at home about school.

Janice brought Louise's concerns to me as the course instructor. Janice was worried that she wasn't a special education teacher, concerned that she might not be able to help Emma and would disappoint Louise. I shared with Janice that we could help Emma and Louise by learning as much as we could about Emma's literacy abilities and behaviors in our program and so provide a different perspective from the school. We would acknowledge that we do not work from a special education framework but that if, in our work with Emma, we found data that pointed us toward recommending a different assessment direction, we would discuss that with Louise. Together we met with Louise to share our approach. With Emma, Janice took a much less direct approach. She recognized through her discussions with Louise and her initial observations of Emma that she needed to proceed more slowly and more indirectly. Emma had been the subject of assessments before and Janice first wanted to establish a sustaining bond. Rather than starting in immediately even with the less threatening interest surveys, Janice decided to spend time talking, reading with, and playing games with Emma.

Janice adapted the Reading Attitude Survey, found in chapter 2. Emma completed several of the sentences but left many blank. For example, she completed the sentence "I like to read about" with "funny book". Her favorite book was Ivy and Bean and during the weekends she said she liked to play. She left blank all the questions about reading at school.

When Emma was reluctant to talk about Mittens, her stuffed cat special object, Janice suggested that they draw instead of talk. Janice sketched her iPhone, which she had brought in as her object, and Emma sketched Mittens. Janice noticed that Emma's body language became much more relaxed when she picked up the crayon to draw. Emma's drawing of Mittens demonstrated great skill. Janice realized that art was an area of strength and comfort for Emma. To get to know her further, Janice brought in a stack of magazines the next week. She told Emma that they were each going to create a collage about themselves with the magazines pictures. Together they cut, drew, and talked. Emma opened up more about herself, and shared her extensive travels in the United States. She also confided in Janice that sometimes she felt "dumb" in school.

Assessment Tools Used with Emma

Janice, Emma's tutor, understood that she needed to develop a more close-grained analysis of Emma's abilities in decoding and fluency. Because Emma's teacher and mother had raised concerns about the possibility of Emma having some kind of learning disability, Janice wanted to assess a range of literacy areas to see if she could begin to uncover clues to what might be preventing Emma from being a strong, grade-level reader.

Sight-Word Assessment

Janice assessed Emma's sight-word abilities in two different ways. First, she played games. They played sight-word bingo, and Janice noted the words that Emma read automatically and those that she could not read. Through playing the game, Janice noted that Emma recognized many of the sight words found on the Fry (1980) list, such as small words, *are, this, the, and* as well as longer ones, *people, more, number.* Janice knew that children's sight-word vocabularies can vary from child to child and so it was important to get a baseline of information. Using index cards with the Fry 100 and second 100 words, she found that out of the 150 words presented (over two sessions) Emma knew 63 words.

Phonemic Awareness

Because phonemic awareness, the ability to hear and manipulate sounds of letters and within words, is a building block of literacy abilities, Janice wanted an assessment of Emma's abilities, even though she was not strictly an emergent reader. She first investigated Emma's ability to hear rhymes, and so would ask her if two words rhymed, such as "cat/hat" or "cat/snow". Emma was able to identify the rhymes, generate rhymes, and identify initial and final consonants.

Running Record

While Emma demonstrated knowledge of sight words, Janice knew if Emma's teacher was reporting a struggle with reading, there might be issues in decoding. Janice again used a multidimensional approach toward assessing Emma. First she used a running record of a text at second-grade level. Emma struggled with the text, reading haltingly. She was unable to retell much of the story.   Janice then used the Informal Phonics Survey (McKenna and Stahl, 2003), which isolates consonant sounds, consonant diagraphs, silent e words, vowel diagraphs, vowel diphthongs, short vowels and R-controlled vowels. This tests words in isolation and the reader's ability to understand word patterns. In this assessment, she performed better than in the authentic text, but inconsistently. For example, she mastered consonant sounds and consonant diagraphs, and some of the more difficult R-controlled vowel words. But she was unable to read any of the silent e words, and missed several short vowel words.

Spelling Inventory

Because Emma was experiencing difficulty with decoding, Janice decided to use a Spelling Inventory to gain insight into Emma's encoding. She used the Words Their Way Spelling Inventory Feature Guide. The data from this instrument showed that Emma understood and could accurately represent initial and final consonants, short vowels, digraphs, and most blends (see Table 7.1). Emma did need work on long vowel patterns and other vowel patterns, such as oi, as well as inflected endings and syllables.

Listening Comprehension

Janice assessed Emma's listening comprehension in two ways—informally and formally. First, she read her *The Memory String*, by Eve Bunting. She told Emma to listen carefully as she read and

Table 7.1   Emma's Spelling Assessment

Emma's spelling	Target word
Flote	float
tran	train
plass	place
prive	drive
prit	bright
shopping	shopping
spiol	spoil
srving	serving
chud	chewed
cras	carries
mars march	marched
shawr	shower
botll	bottle
far	favor
ripin	ripen
salr	cellar
plasher	pleasure
fuchnit	fortunate
kunifit	confident
slvlis	civilize
hopasishn	opposition

then she read the book without interruption or discussion. She asked Emma to retell the story, and noted that Emma was able to relate the main events, characters, and even used some of the vocabulary in the book. This book is at a third-grade reading level. To formally assess Emma's listening comprehension level, she read passages from a commercial Informal Reading Inventory (IRI) and found Emma was able to perform at a fourth-grade level in listening.

Emma's Literacy Profile

Janice found that working with Emma over the first semester was an exciting challenge. While she kept in mind Louise's focus on wanting a "diagnosis" or answer Emma's school struggles, she set about learning as much as she could about who Emma was—as a child and as a literacy learner. She discovered Emma's remarkable talents as an artist. She also found a great gulf between Emma's ability to understand what was read to her and her own abilities to read. While she had some foundational abilities, there appeared to be gaps in her sight-word knowledge, decoding abilities and in her ability to make sense of what she read.

Although Emma grew more open and talkative with Janice as the sessions continued, she also observed Emma's sometimes unpredictable frustrations with different activities. This happened frequently in the community share time in playing games.

Emma's Strengths

- Enjoys listening to stories.
- Enjoys and is skilled at drawing.
- Strong background knowledge.
- Beginning decoding knowledge.
- Growing sight-word recognition.
- Usually very willing to work hard.
- Instructional reading level at second-grade level or Fountas-Pinnell level J; listening comprehension level at fourth grade.

Emma's Vulnerabilities

- Needs extensive support in decoding.
- Listening comprehension is stronger than reading comprehension.
- Difficulty reading aloud extended text.
- Hard to read handwriting.
- Performance can be very variable.

Intervention and Instructional Plan for Emma

Janice created four primary goals for her intervention plan while working with Emma. Her four goals were

1. Strengthen sight-word recognition.
2. Increase decoding skills.
3. Increase motivation and engagement in literacy activities.
4. Develop fluency as she integrates decoding and comprehension skills.

Janice's strategies in each area were:
To strengthen sight-word or high-frequency word recognition:

- Weekly, targeted practice, alternating between games, lists, texts.
- Use of texts that contain targeted words.

To support her growth in decoding:

- Use of consistent sound/word cards to anchor understanding.
- Word sorts.
- Compare-Contrast approach.
- Use of engaging texts that contain targeted words

To increase her motivation and engagement in literacy activities:

- Read an extended text, one that is grade appropriate as a read aloud each week.
- Provide opportunities for Emma to demonstrate her talents among other Literacy Space students.
- Provide positive and supportive feedback when she struggles.

To develop greater fluency

- Echo reading in lesson settings.
- Choral reading opportunities with other students.

Lesson 1

Janice initially had difficulty in determining what to do first with Emma. Because Emma's needs were many, she felt a bit overwhelmed by her needs. In our discussions, we talked about working from Emma's strengths during her time at Literacy Space, such as her strong listening comprehension, to begin to address her vulnerabilities. While we may indeed recommend further testing for Emma, our goal for her time at Literacy Space was to support her development as a reader and learner as best we could.

Janice decided that Emma would work best with a predictable tutoring structure so that each session would have a similar agenda from week to week. This is consistent with interventions such as Wilson Reading System or Reading Recovery, in which each one-to-one tutoring session follows a predictable pattern. To meet Emma's needs, Janice created the following weekly plan:

- Sight-word activity such as Bingo, Concentration, or timed word lists (5 minutes).
- Reading of instructional level text (15 minutes).
- Targeted decoding activity (15 minutes).
- Listening to, discussing, and activities based on a more advanced text (20 minutes).
- Community time (remaining time).

Because of the gap between Emma's instructional reading level and listening comprehension level, she wanted to make sure Emma was challenged to continue to think about texts.

In the initial lesson, Janice began with presenting Emma with a set of sight-word cards that she had personalized for her. She created these out of index cards with a word on one side, and elegant and colorful monogram of Emma's initials on the other. Janice pulled out five words that Emma hadn't recognized before, and that would appear in the text Janice was planning to use in the instructional reading segment of the lesson. Janice and Emma read through the words, and then played Concentration with the cards.

Next, Janice used the book *Days with Frog and Toad*, by Arnold Lobel as an instructional text. She was mindful of selecting a text that Emma could manage with some support and that was also engaging and humorous. Before reading, she took out the cards with the sight words that Emma would soon encounter, to get Emma prepared to see them. She also asked Emma to think about her home chores, and what she thought about doing them. Emma then read the first story in the book aloud, with Janice coaching her as she read. After reading, Emma retold the story and they discussed how Frog helped Toad to get his chores done, almost as trick.

Next, Janice used a word from this story as the basis for decoding work. She selected "right" and worked to elicit from Emma other words that rhymed with it. Janice recorded all the words she said, such as bite and flight. Janice wrote each word on an index card and had Emma sort them.

Finally, Janice brought in two chapter books, *Anastasia Krupnik,* by Lois Lowry, and *The Worst Witch,* by Jill Murphy. Both had strong girl characters and were funny. Janice wanted to enable Emma to select the one she would like to have as a weekly read aloud. By reading to Emma, Janice would model a range of strategies proficient readers use and engage Emma with a text that matched her listening level.

Lesson 2

Engagement and confidence in participating in literacy activities was a particular goal for working with Emma. As the semester neared the end, Janice wanted to provide Emma an opportunity to participate comfortably in the Reading Recital. She suspected that Emma might be shy about reading on her own, and so approached another tutor to plan reading a poem together. Both tutors wanted to support their children in reading with joy and confidence, and the other student, was more outgoing and confident than Emma. They selected the poem, *Good Books, Good Times* by Leo Bennett Hopkins. The repetitive language of the poem along with the rhythm made it a good choice to develop fluency.

Good Books, Good Times
Good books.
Good times.
Good stories.
Good rhymes.
Good beginnings.
Good ends.
Good people.
Good friends.
Good fiction.
Good facts.
Good adventures.
Good acts.
Good stories.
Good rhymes.
Good books.
Good times.

While working through the poem, Emma noticed that poem reminded her of a cheer and that cheering was something she'd hope to do when she got older. Janice took note of this interest and asked Emma and her partner if they could write a cheer themselves. The girls went off by themselves and came up with a chant about Literacy Space.

Learn Students Learn
Read students read.
Fill your minds with lots of stories.
Write students write.
So much fun we never get tired.
Learn students learn.
Time spent getting smarter and smarter.
Teach tutors teach.
Help us learn and feel much stronger.
Learn students learn!

Lessons Learned

Emma performed *Good Books, Good Times*, and the Learn Students Learn at the Reading Recital at the end of her time in Literacy Space. It was the first time she'd read anything in public and her mom and brothers cheered her success. At Literacy Space, Emma found a supportive tutor with whom she could begin to trust to share her own emotions and frustrations around her learning needs. She also experienced a different environment that enabled her to feel supported so that she could grow as a reader in her own way. Emma felt more comfortable as she realized that many children face struggles in reading and writing and she lost some of her self-consciousness and embarrassment about what she couldn't do. She began to learn how to use her strengths in drawing and listening to work on unlocking her struggles with decoding.

While Janice saw progress in Emma's work and especially in her stamina, she also believed that Emma would need more intensive and focused work in the future. Janice learned that in this instance, Emma's literacy needs were complex and at this point, beyond Janice's area of expertise. Janice learned to create tightly structured lessons that targeted a unique learners needs. She learned how to work with a student who had serious needs through supporting her strengths. Although Janice was not able bring Emma up to grade level, nor offer a complete diagnosis and plan for the future, she was able to provide meaningful experiences for Emma and provide her mother with a valuable perspective as she made further decisions concerning her daughter.

All teachers encounter students who challenge their notions about typical literacy development. We learn from this the importance of looking carefully at each child to uncover his or her areas of strength and target those areas of need. We also learn that sometimes it is important to create modest but attainable goals.

References

Al Otaiba, S. and Torgesen, J. (2007). "Effects from intensive standardized kindergarten and first-grade interventions for the prevention of reading difficulties." In S. R. Jimerson, M. K. Burns, and A. M. VanDerHeyden (eds.), *Handbook of Response to Intervention: The Science and Practice of Assessment and Intervention* (pp. 212–222). New York: Springer.

Bloom, F. and Taub, N. (2003). *Recipe for Reading: Intervention Strategies for Struggling Readers.* Cambridge, MA: Educators Publishing Service.

Bunting, E. (2000). *The Memory String.* New York: Clarion.

Connor, D. J. (2011, January). "Questioning 'normal': Seeing children first and labels second." *School Talk: 1–3.*

Demos, E. S. and Foshay, J. D. (2010). "Engaging the disengaged reader." *The New England Reading Association Journal,* 45(2): 57–62.

Dorn, L. I. and Schubert, B. (2008, Spring). "A comprehensive intervention model for preventing reading failure: A response to intervention process." *The Journal of Reading Recovery,* 7(2): 29–41.

Federal Register. (2006, August 14). *Assistance to states for the education of children with disabilities and preschool grants for children with disabilities: final rule.* Retrieved April 19, 2012 from, eddocket.access.gpo.gov

Fuchs, D. and Fuchs, L.S. (2006). Introduction to response to intervention: What, why, and how valid is it? *Reading Research Quarterly, 4(1),*93–99.

Gersten, R., Fuchs, L. S., Williams, J. P., and Baker, S. (2001). "Teaching reading comprehension strategies to students with learning disabilities: A review of research." *Review of Educational Research,* 71(2): 279–320.

Hallahan, D. P. and Mercer, C. D. (n.d.). Retrieved online March 22, 2012 from http://nrcld.org/resources/ldsummit/hallahan.pdf

Hollenbeck, A. F. (2010). "Instructional makeover: Supporting the reading comprehension of students with learning disabilities in a discussion-based format." *Intervention in School and Clinic,* 46(4): 211–220.

Hughes, C. A. and Dexter, D. D. (2011 A response to intervention: A research-based summary. *Theory into Practice,* 50(4): 4–11.

Jensen, D. , Tuten, J., Hu, Y., and Eldridge, D. (2010). *Teaching and learning in the (dis) comfort zone: A guide for new teachers and literacy coaches.* New York: Palgrave Macmillan.

Johnston, P. (2010). "An instructional frame for RTI." *The Reading Teacher,* 63(7): 602–604.

Lose, M. K. (2007). "A child's response to intervention requires a responsive teacher of reading." *The Reading Teacher,* 61(3): 276–279.

McKenna, M. C. and Stahl, S. (2003). *Assessment for Reading Instruction*. New York: Guilford Press.

Mesmer, E. M. and Mesmer, EMMA.E. (2008). "Response to intervention (RTI): What teachers of reading need to know." *The Reading Teacher*, 62(4): 280–290.

Morris, D. and Gaffney, M. (2011). "Building reading fluency in a learning-disabled middle school reader." *Journal of Adolescent and Adult Literacy*, 54(5): 331–341.

National Dissemination Center for Children with Disabilities (NICHCY, 2004). Disability Fact Sheet, No. 7. Washington, DC: NICHCY.

National Joint Committee on Learning Disabilities. (2011). "Comprehensive assessment and evaluation of students with learning disabilities." *Learning Disability Quarterly*, 34(1): 3–6.

National Reading Panel. (2000). *Report of the National Reading Panel: Teaching Children to Read* (NIH Publication No. 00–4654). Bethesda, MD: National Institute of Child Health and Human Development, National Institutes of Health.

Osborn, F., Freeman, A., Burley, M., Wilson, R., Jones, E., and Rychener, S. (2007). "Effect of tutoring on reading achievement for students with cognitive disabilities, specific learning disabilities, and students receiving title 1 services." *Education and Training in Developmental Disabilities*, 42(4): 467–474.

Staudt, D. EMMA. (2009). "Intensive word study and repeated reading improves reading skills for two students with learning disabilities." *The Reading Teacher*, 63(2): 142–150.

8

Julisa, an Early Adolescent Reader

Most of the children who attend Literacy Space are in the early elementary years, between aged six and ten. But sometimes a parent wants to bring an older student, a preteen or tween. Frequently, he or she is the older sibling of the younger child who has been referred to Literacy Space. Julisa was one such girl. Her nine-year-old brother Ernesto was referred and Julisa's dad asked if Julisa, who wasn't doing well in sixth grade, could come along too.

On her first day, Julisa positioned herself at the edge of the hallway, as far away from the door to Literacy Space as she could. At 12-years old, she was in the midst of a tween growth spurt; in the group of small children and adult caregivers, she stood out. Ernesto had easily bonded with another child playing a handheld video game. A bit adrift, Julisa looked as if she wanted to flee.

Nicole, Julisa's tutor came out to greet her. Quickly reading Julisa's anxious expression and withdrawn body language, she understood that Julisa was not ready to enter the room. Instead, she invited Julisa to take a walk around the college. Nicole realized that it would be critical to engage Julisa in an age-relevant activity. She hoped the walk would be an opportunity to learn about Julisa and her school experiences, as they compared the college to Julisa's school.

At first, Nicole found she did much of the talking. Julisa followed quietly as they peeked in classrooms, waited patiently for the elevator, and took a quick sniff at the cafeteria. The last stop was the bookstore. Julisa stopped by the rack of popular paperbacks near the checkout counter. Tentatively she picked up a copy of *Twilight* (Meyer, 2005) and leafed through it. When she noticed that Nicole was watching she quickly put it down and walked away.

Research on Adolescent Readers

Much has been written about the shift at around fourth grade from "learning to read" to "reading to learn" (Allington and Johnston, 2002; Pressley et al., 2001). With increased demands in content-area reading, increasingly complex texts and specialized vocabulary, and the prevalence of high stakes tests, many adolescent readers find themselves struggling. Additionally, some students may have been able to move through early elementary years on the strength of their decoding abilities, where they had not been challenged in comprehension tasks. Others may have been struggling with literacy throughout their school life, without effective intervention.

Estimates of the numbers of adolescent (grades 4–12) students who struggle with reading vary from more than two-thirds (National Center for Education Statistics, 2003) to nearly 40 percent (National Assessment of Educational Progress; 2004, 2005). A major Carnegie Corporation study (Biancarosa and Snow, 2004) revealed troubling facts about student performance such as persistent gaps in achievement between children of different economic and ethnic groups, high-dropout rate from high school, and under preparation of students for college and workplace. The report also revealed troubling gaps of knowledge for teachers, such as lack of training to teach reading comprehension, minimal or ineffective reading comprehension in schools, and the inadequate support for teachers to teach a range of reading strategies to students with a range of differences in reading behaviors. These large numbers of student have caused concern in educational research and called for greater attention toward meeting these needs (Biancarosa, 2005).

However, it is also important to note that there is a range of difficulties that the statistics do not delineate. Buly and Valencia (2002) in their analysis of failing fourth-grade reading scores, found that simply saying failure is not enough, "Reading failure is multifaceted and it is individual...beneath each failing score is a pattern of performance that holds the key to improved reading instruction and consequently to improved reading ability." (p. 232)

Preadolescence and adolescence is a turbulent time developmentally for students. With bodies changing and emotions volatile, students are both more self-absorbed and interested in peers. (Wood, 1997). Students at the beginning of adolescence are easily embarrassed, easily frustrated. Another characteristic of adolescence is expressing resistance and a sense of being easily bored.

Research that includes students' perceptions of school also offers a view how adolescent struggling readers view their struggles. Triplett (2004) describes the frustration and alienation a struggling sixth grader, Mitchell, as he attends a college-based tutoring program. At school, Mitchell is frustrated, especially when he perceives teachers as unable to understand and address his struggles, "It is unfortunate that Mitchell experiences a literacy struggle at school and with teachers. The social comparisons made through reading groups and Accelerated Reader made Mitchel feel dumb. Lack of personal relevance in reading and writing activities made Mitchell feel unmotivated. Relationships with teachers made Mitchell feel fearful, angry, and alienated." (p. 221)

Like Triplett (2004), Dennis (2009) draws upon his experiences in teaching struggling sixth-grade readers to consider frustrations and aspirations of his students and the instructional curricula, defined by state assessment data, that only partially meets their needs. He quotes a student who poignantly said, "Just because I don't always understand what I read doesn't mean I'm stupid" (p. 283). As Dennis looked beyond the test data, he was able to more carefully document his struggling students' strengths to more accurately target their needs. He argues that a one-size-fits-all approach to reading intervention for adolescent readers only serves to reinforce the negative feelings of students and fails to address their unique needs.

Colvin and Schlosser (1998) analyzed efficacy perceptions of successful and marginal literacy students. They found that the struggling students had little confidence in their ability to make progress, avoided literacy tasks because they anticipated failure, defined literacy as isolated tasks, and expressed value for literacy but were uncertain as to how to achieve it. A recurrent theme in their collection of research-based strategies to work with struggling adolescent readers, Moore, Alverman and Hinchman (2000), is the importance of breaking the cycle of failure for older struggling readers. Deschennes, Cuban, and Tyack (2001) illuminate the variety of negative labels teachers have used to identify and talk about struggling readers, such as "disabled," "backward," or "shirker." Explicitly or implicitly, teachers can contribute to this cycle. Dunston (2007) reflects that in her first teaching position she believed, based upon her graduate work, struggling readers had significant deficits that need to be "fixed." As long as she provided them with specific and intense skill instruction, she would be successful. However, she discovered that discrete skill instruction did not address the multiple needs of her students. Her approach then shifted toward uncovering students' strengths and using them to work on areas of need. Hall (2006) in case studies of struggling readers in content-area classes found that struggling readers attempted to succeed in literacy tasks, belying the idea that they were "lazy" but both didn't have the requisite strategies nor had teachers who recognized and built upon these attempts. These studies support a notion that effective literacy interventions for older readers need to address key emotional and attitudinal issues.

An additional factor in the growth of struggling older or adolescent readers is the increasing number of students from culturally and linguistically diverse backgrounds (McQuiston, O'Shea, and McCollin, 2007). These students, much like the English Language Learners (ELLs) discussed in chapter 3, face rapidly escalating literacy challenges in upper elementary and middle school as they are required to tackle more densely worded and poorly structured content-area textbooks. These kinds of texts frequently assume a particular background knowledge and specialized vocabulary that doesn't match that of the students. Other research (Mastropieri, Scruggs, and Graetz. 2003; McCollin and O'Shea, 2005) finds that many teachers lack the expertise of how to development targeted and appropriate literacy instruction for culturally and linguistically diverse students.

What Do Struggling Adolescent Readers Need?

As discussed earlier, it is important to attend to the unique literacy behaviors and needs of each struggling adolescent reader. Houge, Grier, and Peyton (2008) argue that one-to-one tutoring is most effective in engaging adolescents and helping them make gain in literacy tasks. It is critical, they argue, that these tutoring interventions attend to careful assessment as to best identify the specific needs of the student, use well-trained tutors who have the benefit of supervision and are able to create specific lesson plans for the tutoring sessions. In addition, they argue that the incorporation of young adult literature— used in multiple ways (fluency instruction, guided reading, reading aloud, and comprehension)—is a critical component of any tutoring intervention. These texts, relevant, provocative, and engaging, meet the social and emotional needs of the readers in ways school-based texts have not.

Jenkins (2009) describes the suggestions a sixth-grade reader he tutors makes for successful tutoring of an older reader; adults should work as a team to support the reader, build on past success, connect book reading to student's world, allow student to have choice in topics and books, and provide texts on a single topic. Using relevant, diverse, and engaging materials is critical. It is also important, argues Biancarosa (2005), to provide struggling adolescent readers explicit and clear instruction in comprehension. Struggling readers benefit from modeling of the strategies that proficient readers use in making sense of texts. Strategies such as reciprocal teaching (Palinscar and Brown, 1984) provide a clearer road map for the struggling reader. In reciprocal teaching, the teacher models four ways of interacting with the text, questioning, clarifying, predicting, and summarizing. Then students are able to try those strategies with the support of teachers and peers.

At every stage in the process, it is critical to engage the struggling older reader in the process. Adolescents are sensitive to being treated as younger than they view themselves. Those who struggle are especially vulnerable to feeling misunderstood or unacknowledged by their teachers or their families. Moore and Hinchman (2006) urge teachers to:

> Talk with students about their goals and their conceptualization of content and literacy processes. Offer multiple avenues of completions so that students can extend existing competencies in varying ways, suited to their need. Make a point to follow up on individuals' insights. Modify text lengths, tasks, explanations, participation, or even expectations in ways that are pertinent to particular adolescents interests, strengths, and needs. (p. 109)

Addressing Each Struggling Reader as an Individual Is Paramount

Motivation is a central concern in working with older readers. Motivation is, defined by Guthrie and Wigfield (1997), "beliefs, values, needs, and goals that individuals have" (p. 5). Keeping students engaged and invested in reading, especially when they are struggling is critical. There have been, according to Pitcher et al. (2007), two strands of research on motivation and adolescent readers. One area looks at how adolescents are able to create meaning in literacy activities outside of school (i.e., Alvermann, 2001) and another that examines how school privilege print-based texts exclude the kinds of digital and other media literacies with which they have interest and expertise (O'Brien, 2001). Pitcher et al. (2007) developed a survey, in several parts, to assess adolescents' perceptions of themselves as readers, view of reading and readers, and their experiences, in school and out, of literacy activities. This survey contains a multiple-choice section, and a structured interview in which students are asked to give examples and elaborate on responses. As a result of piloting this survey, they discovered several relevant themes about adolescents' perceptions. First, they found that there were often puzzling contradictions between the responses in the multiple-choice sections and the elaborated interview. For example, one student checked that he never reads but offered a detail description, in the interview segment, of several magazine articles he'd read about hunting. Thus, students often didn't identify literacy activities that they chose and that were meaningful to them as reading since they didn't match their school's expectations for reading.

Another theme in this pilot was the use of electronic literacies, and importance of friends and families in students' use of multiple literacies. Finally, choice emerged as key supporting students' engagement with reading. Pitcher (2007) strongly suggest that, "By acknowledging students' reading interests and building on them, teachers can help students expand those interests to related topics over time...Because we know that young people reject literacy tasks that are lacking in purpose and interest, we need to become more aware of students' personal uses of literacy and what is important to them." (p. 395)

Decoding Issues with Older Struggling Readers

Like Moore and Hinchman (2006) we have found that most of the older readers or adolescents who attend Literacy Space do not have significant struggles with decoding. Still, as decoding plays a key role in the reading process and has been acknowledged by the National Reading Panel (NRP, 2000) the role of decoding for adolescents needs to be addressed.

Some, such as Moats (2001) argue that all older readers who struggle, and those who struggle especially with decoding, need extensive systematic phonological and decoding instruction. She states:

> The older student has not practiced reading and avoids reading because it is taxing, slow and frustrating...They cannot read, so they do not like to read; reading is labored and unsatisfying, so that have little reading experience; and because they have little reading experience...Over time, their comprehension skills decline because they do not read, and

they also become poor spellers and poor writers. What usually begins as a core phonological and word recognition deficit, often associated with other language weaknesses, becomes a diffuse, dehabilitating problem with language—spoken and written. (p. 37)

Moats argues that struggling older readers need to be explicitly taught the phonological and phonics foundations that they may not have learned in earlier grades. Successful interventions would "approach language at all levels: sound, word, sentence, and passage." (p. 39)

Salinger (2003) supports this view as well. Presenting older struggling readers with a clearer "road map" to language and strategies to navigate decoding unfamiliar words is essential. With older readers, Salinger suggests, it is important to focus on some of the more discrete difference in words such as flesh/flash or pacific/specific. In response to this kind of instruction, many schools have adopted commercial programs for remediation.

Not all researchers and practitioners believe in the centrality of phonics instruction for struggling older readers. Moore and Hinchman (2006) recommend using Language Experience (Ashton-Warner, 1963), that is, inviting students to dictate narratives and using those texts as the source for instruction about sound and letter meanings. They also advise taking texts from popular culture, such as songs, cards, movie reviews, and driving license manuals to use as the primary source for instruction. Using Words Sorts (Bear, Invernizzi, Templeton, and Johnson, 2004), as we discuss in the vocabulary section and in chapter 3, is another way to support word knowledge in context.

What is critical, as Dennis (2008; 2009) pointed out, is to ensure that only the students who really need targeted phonics instruction, receive it. Because many readers are identified as struggling based on standardized assessments, too often "poor readers" are assigned the same kind of remedial instruction program that typically has a large phonics component (Allington, 2002, 2011; Franzak, 2006; Hall, 2006). Too often, "students are receiving instruction in reading that is often decontextualized and does not provide access to print. Struggling readers are not being provided with books to read." (Dennis, 2008, p. 580)

Vocabulary Instruction

Older readers who struggle often can decode unfamiliar words but struggle with the increasingly diverse and content-specific vocabulary they encounter with more complex and discipline specific texts (Blachowicz and Fisher, 2002). Too often teachers assign students lists of words to look up, define, and use in sentences. In our experiences, vocabulary instruction needs to be tied to texts, iterative, and generative. Because of the quantity of new words students will encounter as they read more and more nonfiction, we need to prepare them to handle new words on their own. The following strategies have worked well with our struggling older readers.

Word sorts (Bear et al., 2004) and as discussed in chapter 3, can be used effectively to support older readers' understanding of relationships among and between words. Typically, a teacher determines a group of 10–15 words that are relevant to a text or topic. The sort can be closed, which means the teacher states the categories to be used to sort the words such words to describe attributes of two different characters in a novel or words deriving from two different roots, such as *astro* and *hydro*. Or teachers can ask students to complete an open sort, in which students create their own categories that enables teachers to glimpse the understanding students bring to the task. This activity can be used at the beginning of a lesson, to assess vocabulary knowledge, or at points throughout, to provide students multiple opportunities to explore and manipulate the words.

Another strategy to use, and one that acknowledges the different knowledge students own and the need to develop metacognitive abilities, is Vocabulary Self-Awareness (Fisher, Brozo, Frey, and Ivey, 2007). In this strategy, the teacher selects words she or he views as important for the text and creates a chart that lists the word and a place for the student to evaluate his or her knowledge of the word (+ for comfortable, a check if unsure, and a – if completely unknown) and areas for examples and definitions. Students are then charged with revisiting and revising their vocabulary lists as they progress with the readings and discussions. This technique supports students in becoming more independent in their learning as well as providing multiple opportunities to work with new words.

Comprehension Strategies for Struggling Older Readers

Overwhelmingly, the majority of older readers who are struggling have significant challenges with comprehension. For some, the challenges are compounded by difficulties with decoding and vocabulary as discussed above, but comprehension is the area in which readers need to pull everything together. Two key elements to support readers are providing them with engaging, relevant, and accessible texts and explicit, guided instruction in reading comprehension.

As noted throughout this chapter, adolescent readers are developing perceptions of themselves as readers. Motivation and opportunities for choice are critical components, in particular for struggling and disengaged readers. It's important to provide options in terms of reading materials. This means a variety of topics, genres, content areas, as well as media. Including digital media is also a key component of engaging resistant readers.

Of utmost importance, is providing older readers who struggle, explicit instruction in comprehension. Since much of the reading older readers do, especially in school, is silent as opposed to oral reading, teachers may make many assumptions about what students can do. When teachers make visible, through modeling and think alouds, what goes on in ones' head while reading, they are able to make explicit the range of strategies proficient readers use to make sense of texts (Duffy, 2003; Tovani, 2000). Duffy (2003) usefully breaks down comprehension into predicting, monitoring and questioning, imaging, inferring, look-backs or fix-it, summarizing, drawing conclusion, evaluating, and synthesizing. He suggests teachers explain, model, and remodel these elements with appropriate texts in meaningful ways to demystify the comprehension process.

Background Tools Used with Julisa

At the college bookstore, Nicole did notice Julisa's interest in the *Twilight* book. She recognized that this was a very popular book with girls of Julisa's age and she wanted to be able to incorporate Julisa's desire to access what other girls her age read into her work with Julisa. While Julisa might not be able to read the book now, Nicole knew she had an important insight into Julisa's interests and goals.

But Nicole wanted to know more. As part of her second session, she gave Julisa the Reading Attitude Survey from chapter 2. But Julisa's responses were so negative that Nicole wanted to get a deeper understanding of what Julisa valued and cared about. She used an interview framework developed with questions based on Pitcher et al. (2007) and Robb (2000) to learn more about her views of literacy (appendix 8-A). Julisa's responses gave her more insight into the complexity of Julisa's attitudes and understandings about literacy. Figure 8.1 shows some of her responses. In this conversation, Nicole learned that Julisa didn't equate her reading online with "real" reading, but, in fact, Julisa did have interests that she did pursue through online reading. She also learned that in school, Julisa primarily used textbooks.

Nicole also spoke several times, informally and through the structured family interviews with Julisa's parents. Her parents related that Julisa had been a fairly successful student in her early elementary years but began to struggle more in fourth and fifth grade. This year, sixth, Julisa had begun middle school, and was floundering. Her mother reported that Julisa had often wanted to stay home, complaining of stomachaches and headaches. Her parents were concerned that Julisa's anxieties about her academic work were the cause of these complaints. Julisa was receiving some extra help before school, but believed Julisa needed more.

---

1. Did you read anything yesterday? Tell me about it.
   Does reading on the internet count? I was reading about Gossip Girls episodes. And also about some other people.

2. What books do you have in your desk or backpack? Tell me about them.
   At school there's the math text book, I have a social studies textbook, and a science text book. I don't like them.

3. What do you think you need to learn to be a better reader?
   Maybe work harder. Learn more words.

4. Are there any books you'd like to read? How did you find out about them?
   Some girls at school are reading Twilight. I want to see the movie and maybe read the books.

5. Do you have a computer at home?
   Yes—my brother and I get turns to use it.

6. What do you like to read on the Internet?
   I go to TV show websites and read about the shows and the people in them. I sometimes look at the news when something big is going on. Once I found this place that showed really cool animals.

Figure 8.1 Selections from Conversational Interview with Julisa.

Assessment Tools Used with Julisa

Special Object

As noted in the opening anecdote, Julisa initially appeared to not care too much about participating in Literacy Space. She was polite but didn't share any enthusiasm or show direct interest in any of Nicole's activities at the first session. She hadn't brought in a special object, like her brother. Nicole shared her object, a picture of her grandmother, and tried to engage Nicole in conversation about her family. But Julisa said very little. Nicole came to her instructor concerned that Julisa might not return to Literacy Space the following week. But the following week Julisa did return, this time with an object. She brought in a photo album of a family trip to Mexico to visit relatives. Julisa became animated when she came to photos of a visit to a beach and photos of fish and sea mammals.

Informal Assessment

Because of the concerns expressed by Julisa's parents about her growing anxiety about going to school, as well as Julisa's own negative feelings about reading in school, Nicole decided it was important to provide some time each week to support Julisa with her homework. While we had made clear to teachers and to families that Literacy Space was not a homework-help program, Nicole and her instructor used short and targeted discussions of Julisa's homework as an assessment strategy. Through looking at Julisa's textbook assignments in social studies and science, Nicole learned that Julisa often did not use the text supports (headings, bold words, key questions, etc.) to help her answer questions. She also found that Julisa's vocabulary knowledge was limited, especially in content areas. Finally, Julisa was uncomfortable in expressing and then supporting her views in the writing assignments she was given.

Commercial Informal Reading Inventory (IRI)

Since Julisa was an older reader, who, through informal literacy activities demonstrated fundamental abilities in concepts of print, decoding, and language and reading comprehension, Nicole decided to use an IRI to gain more specific knowledge about her reading abilities, most specifically, the relationship between her decoding abilities, vocabulary, and comprehension skills. To better plan her instruction and to help support Julisa's academic work, Nicole wanted to be able to identify her independent, instructional, and frustration reading levels. She used the *Qualitative Reading Inventory-4* (Leslie and Caldwell, 2006). This IRI, like others, provides graded passages, both narrative and expository. The IRI also enables the evaluator opportunities to assess both oral and silent reading. For an older reader, such as Julisa, this is important. Finally, in this IRI there are comprehension question probes that assess the reader's ability to recall text, analyze text, and use the text to support his or her answer. Nicole wanted to be able to understand not only what Julisa remembered about what she read, but also what comprehension skills she used.

Using the graded word lists, Nicole found that Julisa's decoding skills were at her grade level. She was able to decode words such as "pyramids" and "moisture," in the sixth-grade list. Yet, after the assessment, Nicole did discover that Julisa was unfamiliar with the meanings of many of the words. Because of this finding, Nicole began her assessment in the passage reading with the fourth-grade selection. Julisa read the selection, one about Amelia Earhart with, only one miscue, and at a steady pace. She was able to retell the main elements of the passage, but struggled with more implicit questions, such as "How do we know Amelia Earhart believed in equal rights for women?" (Leslie and Caldwell, p. 261). Even with looking back at the passage, Julisa struggled. In reading a different passage silently, Julisa also had difficulty moving beyond a literal retelling and was unable to use looking back at the text as a way to support her comprehension.

From this assessment, Nicole determined that Julisa's instructional level was grade five, her independent level, grade four, and her frustration level, grade six.

Standardized Assessment

From her discussions with Julisa's parents, Nicole understood that they had very urgent concerns about Julisa's grades in her new middle school and the implications of her literacy struggles as she moved toward high school. Although Nicole believed that she learned more nuanced information about Julisa through her informal assessments and Julisa's responses to one-to-one instruction, Nicole also understood the importance of analyzing Julisa's performance on standardized instruments, an assessment more typical of the ones Julisa encountered at school. Nicole administered the Group Reading Assessment and Diagnostic Evaluation (GRADE) to Julisa. This assessment was discussed more fully in chapter 3. She gave her assessments in word meaning and vocabulary, sentence comprehension, passage comprehension and oral language. Unlike with Souta, it was important for Nicole to replicate the school context and so she decided to time Julisa in the tasks. However, she spaced these assessments over ten weeks so that Julisa would not interpret Literacy Space as "just like school." She also explained to Julisa exactly what each assessment was about and why Nicole wanted to learn from it. Bringing Julisa into the assessment process both helped Julisa begin to develop a fuller conception of what reading entailed as well as helped her become more invested in the process. Nicole discovered that Julisa wanted very much to understand more about her reading abilities and struggles.

Julisa's performance on the GRADE correlated the scores and finding on the other reading assessments. On the level-five assessment, Julisa scored highest on the oral language, above fifth-grade level, and barely fifth-grade level on the remaining areas, with vocabulary the weakest. When Nicole looked more closely at her test responses, she discovered that Julisa was able to get main idea questions correct but missed those that required inferential thinking.

Julisa's Literacy Profile

Nicole carefully analyzed the data from her observations, interviews, and assessment tools employed with Julisa. She found that although Julisa had adequate skills in reading, the increasingly rigorous demands of middle-school academic work had put a strain on Julisa's abilities and confidence.

Julisa's Strengths

- Aware that texts represent meaning.
- Identifies main idea in fiction and nonfiction texts.
- Accurately answers explicit questions about texts.
- Accurate decoding abilities.
- Motivated to improve her reading.
- Instructional level at fifth grade

Julisa's Vulnerabilities

- Difficulty in answering implicit questions.
- Struggles with using text structures to support comprehension in non-fiction genre reading.

- Difficulty understanding theme, character development questions over extended texts.
- Limited vocabulary and strategies to understand unfamiliar words.
- Reluctance to write.
- View of reading tied only to school.

Intervention and Instructional Plan for Julisa

Nicole created five primary goals for intervention plan while working with Julisa. Her five goals were:

1. Build and expand vocabulary.
2. Increase comprehension abilities in expository texts.
3. Increase ability to move beyond literal reading of texts (inference, themes, character development, etc.).
4. Develop a greater flexibility and willingness to write in variety of genres.
5. Develop a wider understanding and engagement with literacy and development of greater confidence.

Nicole's strategies in each area were:
To develop vocabulary:

- Use direct instruction to support using context clues.
- Targeted instruction with words from the texts we are using.
- Selected words from Tier Two, along with strategies to support learning (Beck, McKeown, and Kucan, 2002).

To increase comprehension in expository texts:

- Using picture and other illustrations to support meaning.
- Graphic organizers to support understanding text structures.
- Begin with materials in areas Julisa has expressed interest.
- Integrating vocabulary work into comprehension.

To increase more sophisticated comprehension abilities:

- Using short texts such as poetry and songs.
- Making connections from television and movies to texts through discussion of more inferential and thematic questions.
- Using novels or short stories with strong, engaging characters, and themes.

To develop flexibility in writing:

- Use journal writing, post-its, graphic organizers, and other tools of "writing to learn."
- Provide opportunity for "real-world" writing.

To increase engagement, deepen understanding of literacy, and build confidence:

- Engage Julisa in the selection of materials.
- Develop a coaching stance to support her independence.
- Use community time to have Julisa take on leadership roles with younger students.
- Integrate web-based texts into lessons.

Based on these goals, Nicole developed a series of lesson plans for Julisa. Because Julisa is an older reader, she wanted to incorporate reading a novel with strong and captivating characters and a relevant theme. This was the kind of work Julisa was experiencing in school and Nicole wanted to give Julisa targeted support to build her skills. Even though Nicole knew that Julisa wanted to read the *Twilight* books, she believed those books didn't provide enough instructional opportunities. Instead, she selected *Rules,* by Cynthia Lord, a novel about the ups and downs of a sister who lives with the challenges of her autistic brother. Her goal was to get Julisa engaged with reading and to support her ability to sustain understanding over a period of time. Novels also provide opportunities for the deeper, inferential analysis she intends to work on with Julisa. Nicole planned to end the semester's work with a lesson on *Twilight* and a gift of the book for Julisa's summer reading.

Because nonfiction was difficult for Julisa yet critical to academic success, Nicole planed lessons in nonfiction strategy development using short, engaging articles from *Time for Kids, National Geographic Explorer,* and from the Internet. She knew she needed to start with shorter, more explicit texts in order to develop Julisa's abilities and stamina in handling the more dense and complex textbooks she was encountering in school. With these texts she could also pull out and target critical vocabulary work.

In planning her lessons, Nicole also wanted to strengthen Julisa's confidence and engagement. She planned to continue to begin with a check in about Julisa's week and work at school. These five-minute chats, Nicole believed, were important to ground their work in having relevance to Julisa's work. The remainder of the sessions would be devoted to focused lessons on vocabulary and comprehension strategies developed within the context of reading *Rules* and then working on nonfiction. Nicole planned to use journal writing, post-its, and other informal writing activities to help Julisa develop her abilities in writing.

Lesson 1

As a way to introduce Julisa to the novel *Rules*, Nicole asked Julisa about what it was like to start a new school. One aspect of a new school they discussed was learning the school rules. Nicole shared that in her experience there were rules that were stated, or explicit, and rules that one understood by experiences, or implicit. She asked Julisa to list rules that she thought were explicit in her new school and rules that were implicit. Through this activity, Nicole's goal was to introduce the idea of explicit and implicit, since reading for implicit or inferential ideas was a reading goal, and a theme of the novel.

The novel starts with a page of rules, written by Catherine, the main character and narrator, for her brother David. Nicole modeled thinking and wondering about the rules and what they referred to as a way to help Julisa understand how good readers think and predict about what they read. Finally, for this initial lesson, Nicole led Julisa on a book walk, to look ahead at the chapter titles (each a rule) and different fonts within the chapter (more rules).

In the following weeks, Nicole engaged Julisa in reading two chapters each week. From week to week Nicole began with the chapter title rule and wondered aloud what it might mean. She reminded Julisa that sometimes writers use these titles to help you understand the big ideas of a chapter. Nicole also introduced Julisa to using post-its as a technique to record her thinking as she reads. At different instances she would model and then ask Julisa to use post-its to record thoughts about characters, and moments of plot tension. Using post-its helped Julisa go back into the text to help her develop her insights about the book and support those ideas with the text. These strategies helped Julisa gain independence and confidence.

Nicole also addressed vocabulary development through the focused reading of *Rules*. She pulled out words from the book that she anticipated would be unfamiliar to Julisa and were Tier Two words. Beck, McKeown, and Kucan (2002) define Tier Two words as those that are useful and important, ones that appear across a variety of domains, have instructional potential, and move toward specificity in conceptual description (p. 19). She engaged Julisa in discussions about those words in the context of the text and used provided activities to promote deeper understanding of the words.

Finally, Nicole used Julisa's informal writings about *Rules*, her journal responses, post-it notes, and other notes, to help Julisa write a more polished piece of writing at the conclusion of reading *Rules*.

Nicole wanted to guide Julisa through the writing process and invited her to think about what would make sense to write about to conclude their work with *Rules*. Together they decided Julisa would write a review of the book and post it to Amazon. This provided a real-world audience for the drafting, revising, and editing of the review.

Lesson 2

Nicole's other strand in her lessons was that of reading nonfiction texts. Drawing upon Julisa's expressed interests in animals, Nicole developed a collection of texts, at a range of reading levels. She knows that it was important for Julisa to work initially with texts that were easy for her to read in order to develop text structure knowledge and stamina in reading nonfiction. Nicole also included magazines and websites in her text set because she knew Julisa valued reading on the Internet but didn't make the connection to literacy.

The first book that Nicole used was *Sharks* by Seymour Simon. Julisa had told a story about seeing sharks while in Mexico and had been curious about shark's teeth and its potential for harm! Before reading, Nicole asked Julisa to list what she thought she would learn in a book about sharks. Then, they previewed the book, with Nicole guiding Julisa to look at the text features. They looked at the table of contents, and Nicole asked Julisa to make notes in her reading journal about what she predicts she would learn in each chapter. As they previewed the book they noted the words in bold and Nicole had Julisa confirm that these words were found defined in the passage and in a glossary at the end of the book. Together they glanced at the photographs, diagrams, and maps, which, especially with the diagram of a shark's mouth, got them both excited to learn more! In this instance, Nicole decided that they would take turns reading. Nicole both wanted to model her thinking and help Julisa monitor her understanding of the texts. As this book was at reading level below her independent level, Julisa was excited to be successful in her reading and motivated to read the increasingly complex materials that Nicole had assembled. Nicole also used the following session. Nicole photocopied a section on sharks from a science textbook at a sixth-grade reading level. This provided an opportunity for Julisa to translate what she had learned about text features from *Sharks* and apply it to the more challenging textbook to secure her learning. This time Nicole invited Julisa, with prompting, to first scan the section to predict, based on the subtitles and captions, what information she would learn from the text. After a discussion of what might be in the text and the passage, Julisa read the passage silently. While Nicole was concerned Julisa might struggle, she believed it was important to give Julisa a supported opportunity to engage in a reading activity typical of those she struggled with in school. Julisa paused at several points and Nicole used those opportunities to ask Julisa what she was thinking. Julisa paused at words she didn't know and Nicole was able to coach her through making a best guess about the word and then confirming it with the glossary.

Finally, Nicole used a Venn diagram graphic organizer to help Julisa organize the information learned from each of the two sources.

When Julisa learned that all the Literacy Space students would participate in the Reading Recital, she told Nicole that she wanted to share something about sharks. Throughout the tutoring sessions, Julisa had always enjoyed opportunities to use Nicole's laptop. She'd once had a peek at a PowerPoint that Nicole was preparing for a presentation in a different course. Julisa asked if a PowerPoint "counted" as work for Nicole's course. Nicole said yes, and invited Julisa to consider creating a PowerPoint to share for the Reading Recital. Julisa was responsible for creating the outline and making decisions about what to share and how, and writing her own "script" to deliver along with the PowerPoint. With great pride and excitement, Julisa was able to stand before her family and the Literacy Space community to present her research on sharks.

Lessons Learned

Nicole's primary focus with Julisa was to develop her comprehension skills so that she could regain confidence as a reader and as a student. She wanted Julisa to develop strategies to read beyond the surface in both fiction and nonfiction. Julisa responded positively to Nicole's consistent acknowledgments of her needs, concerns, likes, and strengths. For Julisa, reading *Rules*, with the accompanying talking and writing, became a pivotal experience. She loved the book, "got" the book, and most importantly, wanted to read another book, "like that one." The extended supports Nicole provided helped Julisa with ability to more deeply understand the more grade appropriate and abstract literacy analysis of them and character development.

In nonfiction reading, Julisa became a more metacognitive reader as she learned to use text features to support her reading of textbooks and other nonfiction texts. By building up Julisa's background knowledge through the use of easier but engaging texts, Julisa was able to tackle grade-level material with greater ease. These activities also supported Julisa's vocabulary development. Using a thematic approach provided multiple opportunities to use words, critical for students to really "own" new words. As Julisa's knowledge, confidence, and engagement grew, she was able to consolidate what she knew in a PowerPoint presentation.

Nicole learned how to approach an adolescent reader with respect for what she brought to the tutoring experience. She quickly realized Julisa's anxiety about being in a class of younger children and revised her plan to address it. This demonstrated Nicole's growing professional development to become a flexible, adaptive teacher. Nicole also learned that her lessons would be more powerful and effective if she drew upon Julisa's interests but provided an opportunity for focused, in-depth work on topics. Rather than moving from text to text, Nicole learned that with a rich, complex, but engaging text such as *Rules*, she could create relevant lessons. She also learned that older students, such as Julisa can be eager learners when they are able to pursue their interests and involved in decision making.

All teachers of struggling readers can learn from Nicole and Julisa. The need for flexibility, to meet students at their areas of strengths and areas where they need additional instruction assures more successful learning opportunities. Julisa initially felt uncomfortable in this learning environment because she was the oldest. Many students come to a new learning environment with the same anxiety, even when their classmates might be the same chronological age. Students, especially as they mature, benefit from having input into their learning. As teachers, we need to see the classroom through their lens and be adaptive in our approaches to learning.

References

Allington, R. L. (2011). "Reading intervention in the middle grades." *Voices in the Middle,* 19 (2):10–16.

———. (2002). *Big Brother and the National Reading Curriculum: How Ideology Trumped Evidence.* Portsmouth, NH: Heinmann.

Allington, R. L. and Johnston, P. H. (2002). *Reading to Learn: Lessons from Exemplary Fourth Grade* Classrooms. New York: The Guildford Press.

Alvermann, D. E. (2001). "Reading adolescents' reading identities: Looking back to see ahead." *Journal of Adolescent and Adult Literacy, 44*: 676–6690.

Bear, D. R., Invernizzi, M., Templeton, S., and Johnston, F. (2004). *Words Their Way: Word Study for Phonic, Vocabulary, and Spelling Instruction.* Upper Saddle River, NJ: Pearson.

Beck, I. L., McKeown, M. G., and Kucan, L. (2002). *Bringing Words to life: Robust Vocabulary Instruction.* New York: Guildford Press.

Biancarosa, G. (2005). "After third grade." *Education Leadership.* October, 16–22.

Biancarosa, G. and Snow, C. (2004). *Reading Next: A Vision for Action and Research in Middle and High School Literacy—A Report to Carnegie Corporation of New York.* Washington, DC: Alliance for Excellent Education.

Blachowicz, C. and Fisher, P. J. (2002). *Teaching Vocabulary in All Classrooms.* Upper Saddle River, NJ: Prentice-Hall.

Buly, M. R. and Valencia, S. W. (2002). "Below the bar: Profiles of students who fail state reading assessments." *Educational Evaluation and Policy Analysis,* 24 (3): 219–239.

Colvin, C. and Schlosser, L. K. (1998). Developing academic confidence to build literacy: What teachers can do. *Journal of Adolescent and Adult Literacy, 41(4),* 272–281.

Dennis, D. V. (2009). " 'I'm not stupid': How assessment drives (In) appropriate reading instruction." *Journal of Adolescent and Adult Literacy,* 53(4): 283–290.

———. (2008). "Are assessment data really driving middle school reading instruction? What we can learn from one student's experience." *Journal of Adolescent and Adult Literacy,* 51(7): 578–587.

Deschenes, S., Cuban, L. and Tyack, D. (2001). Mismatch: Historical perspectives on schools and students who don't fit them. *Teachers College Record, 103(4),* 525–547,

Dunston, P. J. (2007). "Instructional practices, struggling readers, and a university based reading clinic." *Journal of Adolescent and Adult Literacy,* 50(5): 328–336.

Duffy, G. G. (2003). *Explaining Reading: A Resource for Teaching Concepts, Skills, and Strategies.* New York: Guildford Press.

Fisher, D., Brozo, W.G., Frey, N. and Ivey, G. (2006). *50 Content Area Strategies for Adolescent Literacy.* New York: Prentice Hall.

Franzak, J. K. (2006). "Zoom: A review of the literature on marginalized adolescent readers, literacy theory, and policy implications." *Review of Educational Research,* 76(2): 209–248.

Guthrie, J. T. and Wigfield, A. (1997). "Reading engagement: A rationale for theory and teaching." In J. T. Guthrie and A. Wigfield (eds.), *Reading Engagement: Motivating Readers through Integrated Instruction* (pp. 1–12). Newark, DE: International Reading Association.

Hall, L. A. (2006). "Anything but lazy: New understandings about struggling readers, teaching, and text." *Reading Research Quarterly,* 41(4): 424–414.

Houge,T. T., Geier, C. and Peyton, D. (2008). Targeting adolescents' literacy skills using one-to-one instruction with research-based practices. *Journal of Adolescent and Adult Literacy,* 51(8), 640–650.

Jenkins, S. (2009). "How to maintain school reading success: Five recommendations from a struggling male reader." *The Reading Teacher,* 63(2):159–162.

Leslie, L. and Caldwell, J. (2006). *Qualitative Reading Inventory-4.* New York: Pearson.

Lord, C. (2006). *Rules.* New York: Scholastic.

Mastropieri, M. A., Scruggs, T. E., and Graetz, J. E. (2003). "Reading comprehension instruction for secondary students: Challenges for struggling students and teaching." *Learning Disability Quarterly,* 26: 103–116.

McCollin, M. and O'Shea, D. J. (2005). "Increasing reading achievement of students from culturally and linguistically diverse backgrounds." *Preventing School Failure,* 50(1): 41–44.

McQuiston, K., O'Shea, D., and McCollin, M. (2007). "Improving literacy skills of adolescents from culturally and linguistically diverse backgrounds." *Multicultural Leaning and Teaching,* 2(3): 1–13.

Meyer, S. (2008). *Twilight.* New York: Little Brown.

Moats, L. (2001). When older students can't read. *Educational Leadership,* 58(6), 36–40.

Moore, D. W., Alverman, D., and Hinchman, K.A. (2000). Struggling Adolescent Readers. A Collection of Teaching Strategies. Newark, DE: International Reading Association.

Moore, D. W. and Hinchman, K. A. (2006). *Teaching Adolescents Who struggle with Reading: Practical Strategies.* New York: Allyn & Bacon.

O'Brien, D. (2001). "At-Risk" adolescents: Redefining competence through the multiliteracies of intermediatlity, visual arts, and representation. *Reading Online, 4(11).*

Palinscar, A. and Brown, A. L. (1984). "Reciprocal teaching of comprehension-fostering and comprehension-monitoring activities." *Cognition and Instruction,* 1: 117–175.

Pinnell, G. S. and Fountas, I. C. (2010). *Benchmark Assessment System 2, 2nd Edition: Grades 3–8, Levels L-Z.* Portsmouth, NH: Heinemann.

Pitcher, S. M., Albright, L. K., DeLaney, C. J., Walker, N. T., Seunarinesingh, K., Mogge, S., Headley, K. N., Ridgeway, V. G., Peck, S., Hunt, R., and Dunston, P. J. (2007). "Assessing adolescents' motivation to read." *Journal of Adolescent and Adult Literacy,* 50(5): 378–396.

Pressley, M., Allington, R. L., Wharton-McDonald, R., Block, C. C., and Morrow, L. M. (2001). *Learning to Read: Lessons from Exemplary First Grade Classrooms.* New York: The Guildford Press.

Robb, L. (2000). *Teaching Reading in Middle School.* New York: Scholastic.

Salinger, T. (2003). "Helping older struggling readers." *Preventing School Failure,* 47(2): 79–85.

Simon, S. (1996). *Sharks.* New York: HarperTrophy.

Tovani, C. (2000). "*I Read It but I Don't Get It': Comprehension Strategies for Adolescent Readers.* Portland, ME: Stenhouse.

Triplett, C. F. (2004). "Looking for a struggle: Exploring the emotions of a middle school reader." *Journal of Adolescent and Adult Literacy,* 48(3): 214–222.

Wood, C. (1997). *Yardsticks: Children in the Classroom Ages 4–14.* Turners Falls, MA: Northeast Foundation for Children, Inc.

Appendix 8-A Conversational Interview for Older Readers

Did you read anything yesterday? Tell me about it.

1. What books do you have in your desk or backpack? Tell me about them.
2. What do you think you need to learn to be a better reader?
3. Are there any books you'd like to read? How did you find out about them?
4. Do you have a computer at home?
5. What do you like to read on the Internet?
6. Share with the student a book that you've been reading and enjoying. Then prompt student: Tell me about the best book you've read. Ask student follow-up questions, such as how did you know or find out about this book, why was it interesting, and so on.
7. Tell me about something you learned recently from something you've read. Tell me about what you learned and how you've learned it.
8. What kinds of books do you read in school?
9. Tell me about what reading and writing you feel good about in school.
10. Tell me about the kinds of reading and writing that's frustrating in school.
11. Tell me about anything your teacher has done in school that made reading and writing fun for you.

9

Bringing It to Your Classroom

Looking back at my time at Literacy Space, one aspect of those experiences stands out: "The feeling". Once my initial fears subsided regarding the expectation that I would be able to help a struggling reader/writer, I quickly settled into "the feeling" that was created in the space. Surrounded by good literature, games, puppets, quality assessment tools, and caring mentors and peers, I was able to fully jump into my work with a young first-grade girl. I quickly recognized how important my work could be with her. She clearly responded to "the feeling" present at Literacy Space as well.

There were many elements to the structure of our work together at Literacy Space. The support structures put into place assured me that I had all the necessary tools to assess my student's baseline literacy skills as she walked in the door. I was able to take the time to carefully diagnose her particular struggles as I used assessments that determined her phonemic awareness, word-attack skills, comprehension, general attitude about literacy activities, etc. At this time, I also learned the value of informal assessment tools such as conversation to formulate a plan for success. As I sometimes struggled to identify the "how" and "why" of various assessment tools, I was provided support in daily debriefs with instructors and peers. There was always an inquiry approach to our conversations, resulting in well-informed decisions as I made my plans for the next session with my student. Our conversations seemed to always start off with what the student could do, rather than her deficits. Once again, this illustrates part of the powerful "feeling" present at Literacy Space. I was always urged to approach my work by recognizing what the student could do at the time and build from there. This led to a supportive, positive space for all involved. This sticks with me as I think back on the structure my instructors put into place. I believe all decisions lead back to their belief in building on what students already know. We learned to approach assessment in that way.

I have now been teaching for seven years and currently teach second grade. My experiences with that wonderful first grader always come to mind as I encounter a new struggling reader/writer in my class. I think back to how that student would try to deflect attention from the task at hand and how I eventually approached this initial unwillingness. A key activity that made the biggest difference for that child was my decision to use wordless picture books for a while. This was a suggestion given by my instructor, Deb. I had my student tell me the story aloud. In doing this, I learned that she had a wonderful understanding of story structure. I began having her dictate the story to me as she saw it from the picture clues. From there, I typed the story for her and we would read it together. During another session, I cut the story into sentence strips, jumbled them up and we set out to put it in order together. Suddenly, she was looking closely at text with a purpose. She was attempting to read words and began having success because this story was hers. It wasn't long before she wanted to rewrite the story in her own handwriting! Here we were, working with purpose and excitement when only weeks earlier she was very resistant. I believe she lacked confidence and needed someone to take the time to meet her where she was. Today, I look at students like her carefully. What do they know? How can I help them find a purpose as they read and write? I find that most of the time, once students like this find an authentic purpose they are on the path to success.

Yes, I was trained how to effectively use a wide range of assessment tools effectively at Literacy Space. However, what made the difference was learning to take the time and listen to a child. The experiences of my peers at Literacy Space were all different because each of our students were unique and had different needs. We all used similar tools to identify the concrete skills and strategies our students needed. Yet, we all approached our student in different ways. This is my constant goal in the classroom. I have to approach each child differently. How can I create a unique, meaningful, appropriate challenge for each child? My experiences from Literacy Space taught me to take my time and make a personal connection. Having the opportunity to do this with one child developed my confidence. I believe "the feeling" in my room during literacy activities is in large part due to "the feeling" in those magical rooms at Literacy Space.

Sean Moore
Meadows Elementary; Lacey WA.
North Thurston School District.

Becoming a Responsive Literacy Teacher

The immediate goal of Literacy Space for our teachers was to provide an opportunity to test out and make visible, in a supervised setting, the theories and practices they had been learning throughout their Masters' in Literacy Education degree program. Beyond that, it was imperative to prepare teachers with the knowledge and understandings gleaned from their intensive work in a one-to-one setting to meet the challenges that lay ahead. Teachers will be working in rich, diverse classrooms and they need to be equipped with the ability to act as literacy leaders, knowledgeable of new literacy models. "Teacher candidates who are well prepared in teaching literacy are confident in their knowledge of literacy practices and comfortable about effectively teaching reading to diverse student populations in various settings" (Smith and Rhodes, 2006, p. 32). Effective instruction goes a long way in preventing literacy problems and it is the actions of regular classroom teachers that provide the safety net for students who struggle with literacy (Murphy, 2004). "High quality reading instruction is essential in every primary grade classroom in schools with many struggling readers" (Woodward and Talbert-Johnson, 2009, p. 192). Woodward and Talbert (2009) state that quality instruction would minimize the number of students who need intervention or supplementary instruction as well as minimize the number of students recommended for special education. We needed to ensure that regular classroom teachers, the majority of the population of teachers in our master's degree in literacy program, could integrally serve the poor and struggling readers in their own classrooms, instill a joy of reading in all their students, promote active engagement with materials to develop readers, and allow data from assessments to inform their practice.

According to Smith and Rhodes (2006), literacy-method courses provide teachers with background knowledge, the tools with which to recognize students with special literacy needs, and strategies to support struggling readers. As they acquire more knowledge about literacy teaching and learning and have experiences in which to put theory into practice, they realize that they must keep their students' needs at the center of their instructional decision making (Lenski and Nierstheimer, 2006). The best approach to working with struggling readers is to provide high-quality instruction in the first place (Lake et al., 2009). Teachers need to try out instructional techniques, modifying them when necessary by having the opportunity to rethink instruction and student responses (Walker, 2010). Crumpler and Spycher (2006) claim that literacy-preparation programs give teachers the opportunity to use their knowledge of assessment to determine their students' literacy needs to make instructional recommendations. They go on to state, "Effective literacy teachers make decisions access resources, deliver instruction using research-based practices that are tailored to the needs and goals of individual learners" (p. 94). Assessments based on teacher observations yield immediate results and are a means of documenting small changes in student progress. It allows for continuous assessment and provides feedback to facilitate instructional planning (Powers and Butler, 2006). Effective literacy teachers examine all the information they have collected, analyze its meaning in light of literacy development, active reading, and the classroom situation (Walker, 2010).

With the nationwide implementation of Response to Intervention (RTI) as discussed in chapter 7, classroom teachers are responsible for ongoing assessment, instruction, and communication with school-based support teams so that struggling readers are identified and supported before they fall disastrously behind. When teachers have the knowledge of literacy, the experience with a variety of assessment tools, and the flexibility to assess and teach children according to their ongoing analysis of what is happening, the teacher can match assessment with student needs (Valencia and Buly, 2004). "Effective teachers understand the interplay between instruction and assessment and consistently plan instruction based on classroom assessment results" (Powers and Butler, 2006, p. 122). It is that much more critical that teachers have had extensive practice in literacy assessment, "Because the majority of students identified as LD have difficulties acquiring literacy, expertise in literacy teaching and learning is central" (Johnston, 2010, p. 603).

What is essential is a bridge between what teachers learn in both their undergraduate and graduate courses in literacy and the professional challenges of literacy teaching in their classrooms. Too often, a school's professional development program allows for an abstract understanding but is so separated from the classroom that teachers have little opportunity for immediate use. Collett (2012) claimed that a clinical experience allows teachers to develop a disposition toward instruction that focused on interactions within a classroom rather than an isolated understanding divorced from classroom practice. Teachers need to have many experiences to draw upon when considering innovative teaching practices, to reflect on their own instruction, and to develop reasons for teaching as they practice (Walker, 2010). A strong clinical component to the schooling of teachers for literacy instruction is ideal but many teachers do not have the opportunity to participate in this type of experience.

Collaboration with more experienced, effective teachers of literacy and reading/literacy coaches give the less experienced teacher the support needed for pedagogical change. Vaughn and Denton (2008) remind us that it is important for teachers to collaborate with a team or reading coach to interpret data from assessments and to make sound decisions about student needs. Collaboration with other professionals such as those delivering speech and language and English as a Second Language (ESL) help to keep an eye on individual children that can be a challenge in the current environment of accountability and high-stakes testing (Valencia and Buly, 2004). It is also in work with other teachers or a coach that literacy materials can be located and organized that help teachers improve their practice (Blachowicz et al., 2005). Learning communities are created as teachers and coaches reflect on student learning, literacy, and literacy instruction (Walker, 2010).

The International Reading Association (2004) stated, "Reading coaches must be knowledgeable about reading acquisition and development so they can aid teachers in planning instruction that meets the needs of all the students in the teachers' classrooms, and reading coaches must be able to help teachers with classroom assessments that can indicate reliably what those needs might be" (n.p.). The application of new instructional practices is accomplished through discussion. Through thoughtful dialogue with the reading/literacy coach, teachers are encouraged to analyze their instructional decisions (Collett, 2012) and discuss various avenues for developing engaging learning situations for their students (Walker, 2010). It is through dialogue that teachers recognize areas of instruction that need strengthening, together consider alternatives, and reconstruct teaching plans. As teachers work together, they reflect on and maximize the effectiveness of their literacy instruction (Taylor, 2008).

By participating in discussion and reflection with experienced colleagues and coaches, teachers' confidence and competency in literacy instruction becomes more effective. Teams of teachers work together to make use of data to assess students' reading abilities and monitor their progress, adjust their teaching practices to better accommodate their students' literacy skills (Woodward and Talbert-Johnson, 2009). They deliberately cultivate the habit of noticing and observing student learning and the teacher actions that produced it (Walker, 2010). They decentralize instruction in order to appropriately meet the needs of the increasing number of students in their classrooms with literacy needs (Vaughn et al., 2011). Effective teachers of literacy place an emphasis on identifying what students know, their cultural and experiential histories, in order for instruction to build on this knowledge (Walker-Dalhouse et al., 2010). They collaborate, problem solve to increase teacher understanding of how to address students literacy difficulties (Hasbroouck and Denton, 2007). Real, meaningful, and effective instruction unfolds by capitalizing on students' strengths and interests rather than on what they lack, or how far behind they might be from their classmates (Enriquez et al., 2010).

Unfortunately, new teachers frequently discover gaps or disconnects between their teacher-preparation programs and the demands of their specific school or district. They may find that they've been trained to use performance-based assessments but their school relies upon standardized assessments to both evaluate student literacy learning and design instruction. Too often, assessments required by the school districts are not helpful to instruction planning because the outcomes are not shared until months later (Walker-Dalhouse et al., 2010). Historically, schools and teachers favoring a skills-based model for assessment rely heavily on basal texts, decontextualized assessment, and inauthentic reading and writing samples to make evaluations of their students' literacy development (Powers and Butler, 2006). In the culture of these schools, teachers rarely venture out of their comfort zones even when their clinical college experiences with struggling readers gave them new instructional strategies to use.

In some schools, work with a coach can be inconsistent and confusing or nonexistent. It is especially important for teachers to reach out to other teachers to form learning communities around literacy. Work with others can duplicate the supervised clinical experience. It may take the form of coaching as teachers enter thoughtful dialogue about their beliefs, about literacy, and the struggling readers in their classrooms and assist each other in interpreting data, planning instruction, and reflecting on their teaching. Teachers can work together to create a system to monitor students' strengths and vulnerabilities and progress by checklists and rubrics. They work together to overcome obstacles, growing in their awareness of the effects of instructional planning have on the success of their students and their own ability to respond to students' literacy needs (Hasbrouck and Denton, 2007).

Our former student Sean, whose reflection introduced this chapter, now looks at a student's piece of work in depth and can describe what he sees. He is well versed in a variety of assessment tools and knows what information they yield and how to use them. He now recognizes student learning and knows the actions he took to assist the student. From working one-to-one with a struggling reader, Sean has recreated a system of finding individual strengths and interests in the students who also struggling with literacy. Sean, like many of our teachers, has been able to take what he has learned in a supervised, clinical setting and use it effectively in his own classroom.

Lessons Learned from Literacy Space

In order to determine if the lessons learned in Literacy Space were effective for our teachers' classroom practice, we designed an online survey about their experiences. We reached out to all our former teachers for whom we had email addresses and asked them to anonymously respond to eight questions about what they remembered about the work they accomplished with a struggling reader, working with colleagues, parents, the materials to which they had access, and their subsequent changes in educational practice, if any, as a result of the experience. We asked them to reflect on their yearlong program and, having now graduated with a Master's Degree in Literacy, what now "stuck" with them. What did they learn in Literacy Space that echoes in their own classrooms and in their work with their struggling readers and writers? The teachers responded about the materials they still use, the changes in their own instruction, communication they have with parents, and how they feel a stronger sense of professionalism. Below are the findings of this survey with quotes taken directly from the responses.

Materials for Planning and Instruction

As described in chapter 2, the teachers attending Literacy Space had access to a variety of assessment tools, checklists, a large library, games, puppets, and other materials to use when working with their struggling reader.

The use of interest and attitude inventories was found to be important by teachers. They recognized the importance of getting to know their students from a variety of perspectives. "I realized that administering a variety of inventories is worth the time they take in the beginning of the year. They help with differentiation throughout the year," stated one teacher. Another teacher wrote, "I have incorporated many if not all of the personal information surveys: parent/family surveys, student interest surveys and student attitudes and feelings toward literacy surveys. These I found allowed me to get to know my students and families on a personal level at the beginning of the year. I love to see how students' attitudes toward literacy evolve over the year as well." (Many of these can be found in the Appendix.)

Though only a few teachers mentioned specific games, they claimed that they have used them as part of their instructional program or created literacy centers in their classrooms where a variety of games are available to students. After noting the literacy progress made by children at Literacy Space during informal games, the teachers understood the power of learning through play. "The kids think they are playing, but in reality they are also learning and working together." Teachers claimed that reading games helped build reading ability, collaboration, and social skills in their students. Teachers understand the value of games, store bought, teacher made, or from websites. "I believe that students need to be actively engaged and this happens when we use materials that students find meaningful."

In addition, teachers now use a variety of assessment materials with their students, not only the ones supplied or required by their schools but also those mentioned in the preceding chapters as well. Teachers recognized the importance of not relying upon a single assessment and became confident in selecting and using a variety of reading assessments. One teacher stated, "Through my experience in the Literacy Space, I was able to create and carry out individualized learning literacy plans for each of my students. It allowed me to know which assessments may work best for each/all students and how to use them to drive instruction further within whole to small group, along with one-on-one."

Student-Centered Instruction

We identified a general theme in the changes in educational practice our teachers learned in Literacy Space that they brought to their classrooms, one in which getting to know the children in order to proceed with effective instruction was most important. The ability to analyze assessment data to inform instruction was carried over to classrooms. Teachers also expressed a deeper understanding of the struggles readers faced and became more familiar with strategies and approaches to meet those struggles.

The teachers felt that one-to-one time was well worth the time. One teacher claimed it was an effective use of time while another stated, "I left Literacy Space with an understanding that while I must work to support my entire class, I can treat each student like my top priority by working with them individually." Being well versed in an extensive amount of tools and ways to accommodate student needs, teachers learned how to systematically instruct students in a way that scaffolds the students' instruction. Another teacher stated, "Although in teaching we never have enough time for anything we might want to do, I learned that it is essential to make time, even a little bit of time for additional one-on-one time with struggling readers o show them that they are important and that you do care."

Teachers learned the importance of assessment-planning connections; it allowed for theory to be put into practice. "Prior to this program, I did not fully understand how to instruct a student how to read. I was able to identify problems that students were having but I had no strategies to use to help overcome these challenges."

Teachers also learned about alternative instruction from community time, a time when small groups of students worked together completing puzzles, preparing for Readers' Theatre presentations, participating in book clubs, or playing games at the end of each tutoring session. They saw reading as a social experience and shy children entering in conversations, children collaborating while engaged in activities. Teachers learned more about the children by watching them interact with each other and materials. They saw community time as a way to reinforce reading, writing, speaking, and listening.

Working with Parents

Teachers mentioned the five-minute "at the doorway" meetings they had with parents at the end of each session. They remember parents being supportive, receptive, and appreciative. Many mentioned the great relationships they had created with the parents, some extending past Literacy Space. Often nannies and babysitters bring children to Literacy Space, and teachers communicated with the parents through them or through email.

Teachers also mentioned the letters they sent home to parents at the end of each semester and the workshops they delivered to parents during the second semester. They experienced interactions with parents who were involved, interested, and open to learning and supporting their children at home.

In addition, the teachers organized and led parent workshops. They found parents to be open to learning how to support their children's literacy development at home in authentic ways. "I felt my suggestions for how to help at home were really beneficial for the families." Another teacher said, "The parents were very happy and thankful that we were helping their children and them understand more about literacy."

Collaborating with Colleagues

"I am more willing to make time to collaborate with colleagues. I know now that it's a truly a way to work smarter [not harder]." Teachers brainstormed together to solve instructional dilemmas. They enjoyed colleagues' sharing of experience and strategies. They discussed practices they used, materials they found helpful, and shared alternate perspectives. "Fellow colleagues were very open and committed to reflecting on their own experiences, as well as replying and connecting to your own responses. The other students were very neutral and provided positive feedback. You never felt like you were being judged or evaluated."

When unsure about next steps, classmates offered each other advise. They collaborated and grouped together around groups of children with similar needs. They bounced ideas off of each other. They offered suggestions and emphasized with one another's struggles.

Professionalism

"I definitely feel more confident giving and analyzing a reading assessment and addressing the needs of children after assessment." Developing a sense of professionalism, the confidence as a literacy educator, being able to make sound, informed decisions about students' strengths and difficulties, as well as the ability to adapt instruction to meet specific needs was developed in Literacy Space and carried to the classroom. One teacher said she/he was able to transition smoothly from the role of a third-grade teacher to a first-grade teacher with confidence. We read this theme over and over through the surveys hoping that they would become agents for change in their schools.

Applying Lessons Learned from Literacy Space

What our teachers have told us about their new practices in their own classrooms as a result of their participation in Literacy Space, can be valuable for the literacy coach and the classroom teacher. A learning community with access to materials, reflective dialogue, and support can maximize the effectiveness of instruction.

Materials

Many schools have materials similar to those of Literacy Space but are inaccessible or disorganized so are unavailable or not readily available to teachers. One of our teachers said, "Fumbling for materials is the greatest waste of time in a classroom. It shortchanges all the students specially those that need the extra time to succeed." Finding the right materials can enhance and extend instruction not only for the struggling readers but for the whole class as well. Walker (2010), in offering important elements of effective literacy instruction, stated that construction of meaning from various types of materials and in various situations was of utmost importance.

Teachers working together can form a repository of materials on which to draw during planning and instruction. Working together, with help of a literacy coach if one is available, a lending library of materials can be created. A variety of interest and attitude inventories as well as assessments and sample successful lessons, clearly labeled, can be placed in a shared-file cabinet or other space accessible to teachers. A game closet or open bin can hold purchased games and activities. Books for Readers' Theatre, CDs of computer games, and books of instructional strategies can also hold a shelf or two in the closet for teachers to borrow.

Instruction

Teachers must keep their students' needs at the center of their instructional decision making (Crumpler and Spycher, 2006; Lenski and Nierstheimer, 2006).   Many teachers find this to be a tension point in their instructional day since they do not know how to find the time to access each of their student's literacy strengths and needs. Analyzing the data into workable instructional plans becomes an even greater challenge.

For our teachers, becoming familiar with a variety of assessment tools and methods was the foundation for improving their instructional programs. By examining assessment tools in texts, the resource center established using the suggestion above, and in talking to other teachers about the assessments they use, teachers increase their knowledge of how to uncover the literacy abilities of their students. As our teachers told us, the time it takes at the beginning of the year in getting to know the students is well worth it.

Analyzing the data collected from interviews, surveys, and assessments and applying that knowledge to instruction is the key to effective instruction. Instructional help can be targeted, whole class instruction can be better planned, one-to-one guidance can be determined by knowing about individual student's strengths and needs as well as the patterns of student understanding across an entire class. Teachers need to examine all the information they have collected and examine its meaning in the light of literacy development, active reading, and the specific classroom situation (Walker, 2010).

The information teachers discover when analyzing data for individual differences and for patterns of knowledge from a whole class becomes the basis of instruction. Mini-lessons can be planned around themes found in data across all students. Small group instruction can be targeted for students with similar literacy needs. Reading and writing conferences can become specific for each child. It is in this way that teachers' literacy instruction can be most effective.

Working with Parents

Knowing that home-school partnerships are important and putting that knowledge into practice is often intimidating to teachers. A number of studies (e.g., Isenberg and Jalongo, 1997; Shartrand et al., 1997) suggest that teachers are neither prepared to work with families nor are they prepared to implement effective communication strategies with them.

Through regular letters home, newsletters, workshops, and even doorway meetings, teachers and parents have the opportunity to support each other. One of our teachers stated, "I realized that finding the time to send progress reports [that include strategies parents can use at home] every few months is also worth the time. It really pushes most parents to help their children." We have devoted chapter 10 of this book to understanding the importance of developing relationships with students' families and strategies to help foster that development.

Collaborating with Colleagues

Thoughtful dialogue encourages teachers to analyze their instructional decisions (Collett, 2012). Working with a literacy coach or collaborating with experienced teachers and colleagues helps support pedagogical changes teachers want in their classrooms. In working with others, teachers verbalize their thought processes, are encouraged to be reflective of their practice and instructional decisions, and can discuss methods and strategies to implement new understandings and practices.

In some schools, professional development teams are formed by interest and/or grade level. Small groups of teachers meet at regularly scheduled times, often with one teacher acting as facilitator, to tackle some of the challenges they are all facing in their classrooms. Teachers have selected same professional books to read and discuss. They have formed groups to analyze student work, create rubrics, and inform instruction. The topics are limitless. Not all groups are formed through administrative requirements at the school. Teachers can form groups on their own to address literacy instruction, offer support, explore new instructional practices, and to reflect on and maximize the effectiveness of their literacy instruction.

Many schools or school districts have other professionals to whom teachers can outreach. Child study teams, ELL coordinators, parent coordinators, and subject specific coordinators are able to offer assistance to the classroom teacher and may benefit from learning about specific students from the classroom teacher as well.

Professionalism

Our teachers left the Literacy Space experience with a gained confidence as literacy teachers. They had begun to adopt a professional stance, a role of literacy leader, and in some instances, literacy coaches at their schools. Although the Literacy Space experience itself is unique, the lessons learned from that experience are available to all teachers.

Forming professional study and learning groups, entering in professional dialogue with more experienced literacy teachers, and joining professional organizations assist teachers in transforming their perceptions of themselves to literacy professionals. Memberships in local, state, national, and international organizations allow teachers to not only interact with each other at meetings, but give them access to professional journals and literature as well. The International

Reading Association (IRA), National Reading Conference (NRC), National Council of Teachers of English (NCTE), and the College Reading Association (CRA) are just a few of the specialized professional organizations accessible to teachers. We encourage teachers' participation in professional organizations.

References

Blachowicz, C. L. Z., Obrochta, C., and Fogelberg, E. (2005). "Literacy coaching for change." *Educational Leadership*, 62(6): 55–59.

Collett, V. (2012). "The gradual increase of responsibility model: Coaching for teacher change." *Literacy Research and Instruction*, 51(1): 27–47.

Crumpler, T. P. and Spycher, E. (2006). "Assessment has a dual purpose in teacher preparation programs." In S. D. Lenski, D. L. Grisham, and L. S. Wold (eds.), *Literacy Teacher Preparation: Ten Truths Teacher Educators Need to Know* (pp. 92–101) Newark, DE: International Reading Association.

Enriquez, G., Jones, S. and Clarke, L. W. (2010). "Turning around our perceptions and practices, then our readers." *The Reading Teacher*, 64(1): 73–76.

Hasbrouck, J. and Denton, C. A. (2007). "Student focused coaching: A model for reading coaches." *The Reading Teacher*, 60(7): 690–693.

International Reading Association. (2004). *The Role and Qualifications of the Reading Coach in the United States*. Position Statement. Newark, DE: Author.

Isenberg, J. P. and Jalongo, M. R. (1997). *Creative Expression and Play in Early Childhood*. Englewood Cliffs, NJ: Prentice Hall.

Johnston, P. (2010). "An instructional frame for RTI." *The Reading Teacher*, 63(7): 602–604.

Lake, C., Davis, S., and Madden, N. A. (2009). "Effective programs for struggling readers: A best evidence synthesis." Retrieved April 7, 2012 from www.bestevidence.org/word/strug_read_jun_02_2010.pdf. Baltimore, MD: Johns Hopkins University Center for Data-Driven Reform in Education.

Lenski, S. D. and Nierstheimer, S. L. (2006). "Teacher preparation programs offer targeted field experiences in literacy." In S. D. Lenski, D. L. Grisham, and L. S. Wold (eds.), *Literacy Teacher Preparation: Ten Truths Teacher Educators Need to Know* (pp. 44–52). Newark, DE: International Reading Association, 44–52.

Murphy, J. (2004). *Leadership for Literacy: Research-Based Practice, Prek-3*. Thousand Oaks, CA: Corwin Press.

Powers, S. W. and Butler, B. (2006). "Investigating connections between teacher beliefs ad instructional practices with struggling readers." *Reading Horizons*, 47(2): 121–157.

Shartrand, A. M., Weiss, H. B., Kreider, H. M., and Lopez, M. E. (1997). *New Skills for New Schools: Preparing Teachers in Family Involvement*. Retrieved January 6, 2009, from http://www.ed.gov/pubs/NewSkills/title.html.

Smith, K. E. and Rhodes, C. S. (2006). "Teacher preparation programs make a difference in teacher candidates' perspectives about literacy teaching." In S. D. Lenski, D. L. Grisham, and L. S. Wold (eds.), *Literacy Teacher Preparation: Ten Truths Teacher Educators Need to Know* (pp. 32–43). Newark, DE: International Reading Association.

Taylor, B. M. (2008). "Tier 1: Effective classroom reading instruction in the elementary grades." In D. Fuchs, L. S. Fuchs, and S. Vaughn (eds.), *Response to Intervention: A Framework for Reading Educators* (pp. 5–25). Newark, DE: International Reading Association.

Valenica, S. W. and Buly, M. R. (2004). "Behind test scores: What struggling readers really need." *The Reading Teacher*, 57(6): 520–531.

Vaughn, S. and Denton, C. A. (2008). "Tier 2: The role of intervention." In D. Fuchs, L. S. Fuchs, and S. Vaughn (eds.), *Response to Intervention: A Framework for Reading Educators* (pp. 51–70). Newark, DE: International Reading Association.

Vaughn, S., Hughes, M. T., Moody, S. W., and Elbaum, B. (2011). *Grouping Students Who Struggle with Reading*. Retrieved February 1, 2012, from www.readingrockets.org.

Walker, B. J. (2010). *Literacy Coaching: Learning to Collaborate*. Boston, MA: Allyn & Bacon.

Walker-Dalhouse, D., Risko, V. J., Lathrop, K., and Porter, S. (2010). "Helping diverse struggling readers through reflective teaching and coaching." *The Reading Teacher*, 64(1): 70–72.

Woodward, M. S. and Talbert-Johnson, C. (2009). "Reading intervention models: Challenges of classroom support and separated instruction." *The Reading Teacher*, 63(3): 190–200.

Involving Parents, Caregivers, and Families

Mr. Mercedes was a hardworking parent of two elementary school boys. He held two jobs in order to keep a roof over their heads, food on the table, and clothes on their backs. His wife watched a neighborhood infant for extra money but her job was to take care of the boys and their home. Neither had any formal education and we suspected that neither parent had finished high school. They were concerned about their boys' education but did not know how to gain access to services in the school. They also did not know how to help them when each began to struggle with their schoolwork.

Mrs. Mercedes was sharing her concern about her youngest son Miguel to one of his friends' mothers. She explained that Miguel and his older brother were struggling with reading, hated books, and she was at a loss of what to do. It was from this woman that she heard about Literacy Space. Mr. Mercedes made the initial call to us. We sent off an application and we admitted Miguel and his brother Joseph to our program the following semester.

Mrs. Mercedes always brought the boys to the weekly sessions. Miguel's tutor and Joseph's tutor kept Mrs. Mercedes informed of what they were doing at the "door way" each week. But it was through parent interviews that the tutors developed a better idea of the literacy experiences the boys received at home. They learned Mrs. Mercedes's perception of their struggles and strengths, their likes and dislikes, home responsibilities, and personalities. The tutors learned how passionate the Mercedes were about their boys' future achievement. It was curious to them why the Mercedes weren't reading to their boys or accessing the services their public school had to offer but they used Mrs. Mercedes's comments about the boys' interests and selected materials and books that seemed to match as well as books they thought would be culturally relevant.

Mrs. Mercedes attended Family Games Night the end of the first semester with a new perspective on literacy. She never realized that reading and writing could be fun activities at home and at school and had lots of questions about other things she could be doing with the boys at home. She was one of our most interested parents attending the workshops the second semester.

Mr. and Mrs. Mercedes came to the final Reading Celebration at the end of the yearlong program. It was a sacrifice for Mr. Mercedes to arrange his working schedule to attend but he was overwhelmed by the accomplishments of his children. The Mercedes family left our program with an expanded view of literacy and their own family literacy events. They all realized reading could be fun and were all the more motivated to share reading activities together.

Home-School Partnerships

The importance of home-school partnerships as key to student achievement cannot be underestimated (e.g., Briggs et al., 1997; Lazar et al., 1999; Martin and Hagan-Burke, 2002). Faced with increasingly diverse populations, teachers face many challenges when trying to form partnerships with parents. According to Villegas and Lucas (2002), teachers must see all students, including children who are poor, marginalized, and speakers of languages other than English, as learners who already know a great deal and who have experiences, concepts, and languages that can be enhanced and expanded to help them become more proficient learners. Knowing that the educational achievement levels of students from diverse backgrounds lag behind their white counterparts (Vang, 2006) should be motivation enough for teachers to find ways to be more responsive to their diverse classroom populations but many report that they do not know how to work with families (e.g., Larocque, 2011; Shartrand et al., 1997).

The established research on family literacy (Auerbach, 1995; Moll et al., 1992; Taylor, 1983) reminds teachers: that children have learning experiences and a network of people who support various kinds of learning; that children have "funds of knowledge" that teachers rarely draw upon for use inside the classroom. Literacy begins and develops through engaging experiences in homes. "In developing our partnership with families, we are not trying to impose our vision of literacy but to develop relationships with families where we could learn about what already existed in the families and connect with that literacy classroom community" (Moll et al., 1992, p. 94). Auerbach (1995) posits that family involvement programs represent either a deficit or a wealth view of families, either blaming parents for their lack of involvement or acknowledging family resources that can enhance children's literacy development. She suggests that there is evidence that many low-income, minority, and immigrant families cultivate rich contexts for literacy development. Affirming and valuing the many ways in which families share literacy are just as important as introducing new ways for families to experience literacy events (Paratore, 1995).

Parents can provide valuable insights into their children's needs as well as family background, health history, physical and cognitive development. Interviews and conversations can yield information about how their children feel about their own literacy, how they learn, their perception of the child's literacy needs, and when they believed the child started to struggle. Parents see their children in multiple settings, learning in different ways other than those in school. Families' cultural values and existing practices need to be recognized by teachers and built into family programs. For example, Loera and colleagues (2011) report a study done in 2001 by Lopez in which Latino parents viewed communicating a good work ethic to their children was a means of being involved and preparing them for success in school. Loera and colleagues conducted workshops for parents that connected reading achievement with professional jobs to link the two views of parental involvement together.

The relationship, then, needs to be two-way communication and not one where teachers seek to train parents to duplicate school practices. Parents and teachers need to become teammates (Endrizzi, 2008) working together to unravel the literacy difficulties children may be experiencing and finding ways to work in harmony in helping children succeed. Conversations need to be ongoing. Parental support needs to be enlisted. Home should not be turned into school but rather be a place where parents supply support and encouragement and where children can experience success in the usual home literacy events.

Parents are a child's earliest and most important literacy role models (Jennings et al., 2006). A family's contributions to their children's literacy development extend beyond their immediate impact on discrete beginning literacy skills (Dail and Payne, 2010). Children's general attitude and motivation toward reading are developed in the home as well. "Children raised in homes that were predominately oriented toward the view that literacy is a source of entertainment were more advanced in their development of reading related competencies than children raised in homes where literacy was more typically viewed as a set of skills to be acquired" (Baker, 2003, p. 91). If the child, as well as the parent, sees reading as a set of skills or mechanics, then reading is an unpleasant, unrewarding experience. Where parents present reading as a fun activity, one in which they themselves engage, children's reading engagement increases. Teachers should not assume that parents know how to help struggling readers. Working with parents to discover children's interest, the teacher can inform parents about a variety of materials likely to capture the interests of struggling and unmotivated readers (Baker, 2003) and help them to build activities in the already set family routines. Storybook reading plays an important role in providing reading motivation and helps to create a climate where reading is enjoyable. Sonnenschein and Munsterman (2002) found that teachers frequently urge parents to read with their children but provide little guidance about the interactions, which occur around books. They go on to state that the affective quality around reading interactions is important to fostering motivation in reading. This is especially important for children who struggle with reading because if it is not happening in the home, teachers need to create affectively positive book experiences in the classroom.

Sometimes it is not clear what the parents' role should be (Larocque et al., 2011) and teachers tend to lump parents into the group who participates and the group that does not. Parents do not participate in the same ways; some will have more of a presence than others. Low-income parents are not involved in the typical ways that schools expect, nor can they access services to benefit their children (Bolivar and Chrispeels, 2011; Loera et al., 2011; Vang, 2006). Fullan (2001) stated whether or not parents have a terrific or terrible job, they have a vested interest in their children's future and success. Yet, many parents feel intimidated by the professional language of the school and this becomes more evident with parents of children with various disabilities (Larocque et al., 2011). The language is so academic and scientific it seems impersonal that requires the teacher to be the translator and sensitive to the needs of the parents. Parents benefit from brief, straightforward descriptions of their children's struggles and strengths. They need to understand that work with struggling readers may be slow. Parental expectations need to be realistic. Working with parents, Flippo (2003) stated, "Their continuing understanding of the child's work, strategies, goals, and needs, and your assessment and evaluation system, are very important to your success and the child's" (p. 233). Children who struggle with reading are in special need of the partnerships that parents and teacher can create around literacy. Making parents aware of what is happening in the classroom and encouraging them to help their children at home, and being sensitive to and involving home literacy activities in classroom instruction will reinforce and multiply instructional effectiveness. "Struggling readers need teachers who are committed to reaching out to parents" (Jenkins, 2009, p. 161). Parents need to know the difficulties their children are having and need to be informed that there are many bright children who struggle with reading. "Many parents of poor readers and writers are frightened and dismayed by their child's inability to acquire these critical abilities" (Lipson and Wixson, 2003, p. 87). Parents may blame themselves thinking they have caused the problem or that their children are not bright. Other parents blame the school.

Parents' Participation at Literacy Space

Parents make a yearlong commitment to the Literacy Space program. For two semesters, they pick their children up from a variety of public and private schools in Manhattan, the Bronx, Brooklyn, and Queens and make the journey to the college by bus, subway, or car. The commute is not easy but clearly demonstrates the concern they have for their children's struggles with literacy.

In order to create the home-school partnerships we believe are so important for our success, we made efforts to foster relationships with families though interviews, hold family games nights to demonstrate that literacy learning can be fun, keep door of communication open by having weekly conversations with parents and sending letters home at the end of each semester, holding workshops for parents, and ending our program with a Reading Celebration as described in chapter 2. We recognize that the parents were the child's first teachers and possess valuable information to share with us as a first step in assessment and intervention.

Fostering Relationships

Involvement with families provides rich opportunities to learn about and appreciate the literacy teaching and learning children have experienced in their homes (Endrizzi, 2008). During the first few sessions of Literacy Space, teachers sit down with parents and begin to establish a working relationship. Parent interview forms are used to guide the initial conversations (see appendix 10-A and 10-B). We have found many parent interview forms but the two presented here are different from each other. By using a search engine such as Google, a variety of parent interview forms can be obtained.

We adapted the parent interview form in appendix 10-A from Jennings and her colleagues (2006). It is divided into sections asking questions about the home, school, social and cultural environments, physical, emotional, and language development, and space for comments and suggestions. We do not advocate using the entire form at one sitting unless the conversations are comfortable and take a natural turn to many of these areas. As teachers, we need to be sensitive to parental concerns and to their privacy. We do not want to pry or make the parent feel uncomfortable during the initial conversations.

It is possible to take the form and tailor it, adding or subtracting from the questions posed. What we especially like about this form is the initial question, "Can you tell me three positive things about your child?" This question begins to focus on the strengths and good qualities of the child. When working with struggling literacy learners and their families, the tendency to focus on inadequacies of the child is far too prevalent. If parents already feel that they are to blame for their children's literacy struggles or perhaps their children are not capable, by beginning the conversations on what the child does well sets a positive tone for a partnership.

The parent interview form in appendix 10-B is a shorter, less intrusive guide for initial conversations. It asks the parent for their perceptions, observations, and knowledge of their child. The questions are very open-ended with the focus on information seeking. It asks what the parent thinks and notices about the child. It invites the parents to ask questions and to share the child's interests, medical history, or anything else the parent thinks would be helpful for the teacher to know.

Family Game Night

As described in chapter 2, we have a closet full of games for teachers and children to use during their time at Literacy Space. Children enjoy playing the games while employing and improving their literacy skills. It is important to share this aspect of literacy learning with families. Our goal of Family Games Night is for families to engage in games designed by the teachers, targeted at an area of struggle for the child, and have fun.

Toward the end of the first semester, teachers have set goals for intervention that they will plan for and then implement during the second semester. With these goals in mind and with the knowledge of the child's interests, teachers construct a game to play at Family Games Night and one that the child will take home and keep. Teachers have designed games for their children such as board games or card games.

Jillian had been working with Isabella for a semester and knew her love of horses. She also knew that Isabella was struggling with the silent /e/ at the end of words, had trouble reading words with silent consonants such as h and k, and had a small sight word vocabulary for her grade level. She designed a board game that combined her interest and needs in a board game described below.

To the Stable Board Game

Goal: To get your horse back to the stable with three apple cards, five bales of hay, and three buckets of water.

Games Pieces: Playing Board (made out of oak tag), one die, plastic horses (which can be purchased at any dollar store), and three sets of cards (apples, hay, water buckets).

The Game Board: Made out of oak tag, spaces were marked in a pathway that wove around the board. The Start began at the top of the board and the Finish was at the bottom and looked like the entrance to a horst stable. In the center of the board were three rectangles to hold three sets of cards (apples, hay, water). On various spaces were instructions to select one of the cards, special instructions such as "Your horse won a ribbon in the local 4H club show. Move ahead two spaces," or "You forgot to clean out the stall. Lose a turn," or could be blank.

The Cards: Cards were constructed from 4×6 index cards cut in half vertically. One side of the card was either an apple, bale of hay, or bucket of water. On the reverse side was a horse fact question from Isabella's reading, a Cloze activity that required her to fill in the blank with a word in a CVC (consonant-vowel-consonant) silent /e/ pattern, a sentence containing a word with a silent consonant, or other skill related questions addressing her needs.

How to Play: Players select a plastic horse and put it at the start. Rolling a die, they move the horse the corresponding number of spaces and follow the directions on the space. If the space instructs them to select a card, the player selects the corresponding card. If answered correctly, the player keeps the card; if not, the card goes to the bottom of the pile. It is then the next players turn. Game continues as players move along the pathway to the stable collecting cards. The first player to the stable with the correct amount of apples, hay, and water is declared the winner. If a player gets to the barn without the correct number of items, then the player with the most correct number of items after everyone has reached the barn is the winner.

The game was a big hit with Isabella and her family. It employed her love of horses and the skill areas that needed improvement. After Family Games Night, Isabella brought the game home to continue to play with her family.

Max was working on vocabulary with his student, Diego. He used index cards to create a Concentration game that matched synonyms, such as required and needed, benevolent and kind, and fortunate and lucky.

The games described above can be adapted to any interest and tailored to meet the instructional needs of the child. David made Omar a rather intricate Ninja game board employing all sorts of facts about Ninjas. Brittany made a game around Rebecca's cat Oreo. We encourage students to use suggestions found in Padak and Rasinski (2008), websites such as www.readwritethink.org, and their own imagination. The possibilities are endless.

Family Games Night is an evening that connects home and school. It provides an informal opportunity for tutors to work with their children and their families in a relaxed yet instructional setting. We use our literacy abilities to play games that require reading and writing, one of the aspects of Literacy Space that makes it successful. By holding Family Games Night on the last day of the first semester, we are also building in an activity to keep the children involved with their families over the long break between semesters.

Conversations and Letters

It is only through continuous conversations with parents that we know if our interventions are working outside of Literacy Space. Each week teachers meet the parents and children outside of Literacy Space in a small alcove and escort the children into our space. After the session is over, teachers escort the children back to their parents. In each of these doorway meetings, parents and teachers have the opportunity to chat informally about the children. Often, it is at these meetings that parents share news with us. This can be about the family, about the child outside of school, and about the struggles and accomplishments the child is having inside school.

We do not communicate with the children's teachers on a continuous basis. At the end of each semester, we do send the teacher a letter to keep him or her aware of the assessments we have used, data we have yielded from the assessments, interventions we have planned and implemented, books and materials we have used, and what we have suggested to the parents. It is a one-way communication, recognizing busy lives of teachers. More about those letters can be found in chapter 2.

At these doorway meetings, the parent might mention that the child had a difficult day at school or that the child had missed school recently because of illness. We find out about vacation plans, new siblings, added interests, birthdays, and accomplishments in and out of school. Parents might bring in the child's report card to share with the teacher.

It is also a time for the teacher to share what he or she has learned about the child during the session, the books and materials used, and growth or struggles in literacy noticed that week.

Not all parents can attend each week with their children. Children from the same school may arrive together each week with one parent sharing the responsibility of getting them there and back. Working parents often rely on babysitters or older siblings to bring the children to Literacy Space. Teachers may send home notes or interview forms with the child for the parent. Sometimes they come back, sometimes they don't. Weekly, at the doorway meetings are not possible with all parents.

At the end of each semester, the teachers send a letter home to the parents. In some cases where the parents of the child do not live together, each parent is sent a copy of the letter. It summarizes the work done over the semester and suggests activities and books to use with the child to further develop his or her literacy learning. The letter follows a format and is written in parent-friendly terms.

The two letters sent to the parents are similar. Each letter begins with a positive note about the child. The teacher then outlines the results from a variety of assessments done during the semester. These results include both the child's strengths and areas of need. The teacher goes on to describe the intervention used during the semester. The teacher will describe what seemed to work with the child, improvements that were noted. The letter ends with suggestions for the parents to further literacy learning in the home: games, websites, types of books and at what level the child enjoys, home literacy events that are important. The first letter always gives the start date for the second semester while the letter at the end of the second semester, the final semester, thanks the parents for bringing the child during the year and wishes them well. We shared an example of this kind of letter in chapter 2.

Workshops

During the second semester of Literacy Space, teachers work in pairs to deliver workshops to the parents during regular sessions. Topics vary but come from the teachers' conversations with parents. Through the doorway meetings teachers find a pattern to the concerns parents have about what they could be doing at home to help their children with literacy learning, questions about standardized testing, or curriculum. Topics are also generated by the teachers around patterns of literacy intervention needs they see among the children.

Teachers design their workshops around these concerns and questions. However, we require that each workshop include an opportunity for parental sharing of home events and that each parent go home with materials of some kind. These can take a variety of forms including a list of websites, books, a bookmark with questions to ask during a book share, and so on. They also need to give the parents the opportunity to evaluate the workshop so teachers learn from parents what they found useful.

A schedule of workshop dates and topics is given to all parents and posted outside Literacy Space. (see the sample flyer below in figure 10.1). As pairs of teachers work with parents, the teachers' tutees work with other teachers and children for the session.

Although most of our teachers are nervous about giving workshops, they have found that they are gratefully received. Teachers learn how important it is to connect with parents at this level of interaction. They learn how to give the respect to parents that they deserve and appreciate. Parents do not have opportunities to share and learn in an informal, risk-free manner with their children's teachers. Workshops afford them this chance. It further enhances the home-school connection.

Parent Workshops
Wednesdays during
Literacy Space

March 21
What Else Can You Read?

March 28
Comprehension Is Crucial

April 4
Finding the "Just Right" Book

April 25
There's Literacy All Around Us

Please plan on
attending these
important workshops!

Figure 10.1   Workshop Flyer.

Reading Recital

How do you end a yearlong tutoring program? How do you bring together the children, families, and teachers of Literacy Space into a grand finale? For us, it means a celebration of the accomplishments we have seen over the course of the year.

As described in chapter 2, the Reading Recital is a time for the children to share their reading and writing accomplishments in a variety of ways. We have ended many of the struggling readers' chapters describing the finished pieces the children developed to share during their performances.

For parents, this may be the first time that their children have the opportunity to publically share their literacy milestones in a public forum. Over the course of the year, parents have worked with us by providing information about their children during formal interviews and doorway conversations. Parents have learned with us during

Family Games Night and by participating in workshops. Parents have learned from us in the letters they received at the end of each of the two semesters. The Reading Recital is a time for the community of Literacy Space to come together and celebrate the children's and teachers' commitment to learning.

The children create their own invitations to their families. The teachers collaboratively with the children and each other create the program, practice with the children for the night of their performance. As instructors, we set up the room to model a theatre, and everyone brings refreshments. The families come equipped with video and still cameras to document the occasion. We present the children certificates that highlight their unique accomplishments during their time at Literacy Space. We also acknowledge our partnership with the families; parents receive certificates as well for making the commitment of bringing their children to Literacy Space each week. It is a night to celebrate the strong bonds formed, the literacy progress we see in the children, and the teachers' new understandings of literacy acquisition.

This night actualizes the many goals of Literacy Space we describe in chapter 1. Over the course of a year, we have helped the teachers become responsive to the children they tutor by learning about them and about their families. The teachers leave Literacy Space with a multidimensional approach to assessment and instruction. The teachers have tailored the assessments they used to the individual children based on data they collect and analyze. They now understand the limitations of one-size-fits-all standardized testing and look for alternate methods of data collection. They know how to use assessment data to inform instruction, the cyclical nature of assessment and instruction.

The teachers are committed to reaching out to parents, to colleagues, and other professionals for support. The physical environment created in Literacy Space supported ongoing dialogue among all participants, inviting support and mutual problem solving, encouraging creative instructional plans based on the interests of children.

Throughout this book, we have taken the reader through our philosophical and theoretical perspectives underlying our work with struggling readers. We have shared what we have found to be most effective with struggling readers, reasons why children may have difficulty with literacy acquisition, and how and what we do in a small space with children, teachers, and families. We believe in today's diverse and challenging classrooms, teachers and families need to work together to ensure the success of struggling readers.

References

Auerbach, E. R. (1995). "Which way for family literacy: Intervention or empowerment?" In Lesley Mandel Morrow (ed.), *Family Literacy: Connections in Schools and Communities* (pp. 287–303). Newark, DE: International Reading Association, Inc.

Baker, L. (2003). "The role of parents in motivating struggling readers." *Reading & Writing Quarterly*, 19(1): 87–106.

Bolivar, J. M. and Chrispeels, J. H. (2011). "Enhancing parent leadership through building social and intellectual capital." *American Educational Research Journal*, 48(1): 4–38.

Briggs, N., Jalongo, M. R., and Brown, L. (1997). "Working with families of young children: Our history and future goals." In Joan P. Isenberg and Mary Rench Jalongo (eds.), *Major Trends and Issues in Early Childhood Education: Challenges*, Controversies and Insights (pp. 56–70). New York: Teachers College Press.

Dail, A. R. and Payne, R. L. (2010). "Recasting the role of family involvement in early development: A response to the NELP report." *Educational Researcher*, 39(4): 330–333.

Endrizzi, C. K. (2008). *Becoming Teammates: Teachers and Families as Literacy Partners*. Urbana, IL: National Council of Teachers of English.

Flippo, R. F. (2003). *Assessing Readers: Qualitative Diagnosis and Instruction*. Portsmouth, NH: Heinemann.

Fullan, M. (2001). *The New Meaning of Educational Change*. New York: Teachers College.

Jenkins, S. (2009). "How to maintain school reading success: Five recommendations from a male struggling reader." *The Reading Teacher*, 63(2): 157–162.

Jennings, J. H., Caldwell, J., and Lerner, J. W. (2006). *Reading Problems: Assessment and Teaching Strategies*, 5th ed. Boston, MA: Pearson.

Larocque, M., Kleiman, I., and Darling, S. M. (2011). "Parental involvement: The missing link in school." *Preventing School Failure: Alterative Education for Children and Youth*, 55(3): 115–122.

Lazar, A., Broderick, P., Mastrilli, T., and Slostad, F. (1999). "Educating teachers for parental involvement." *Contemporary Education*, 70(3): 5–10.

Lipson, M. Y. and Wixson, K. K. (2003). *Assessment & Instruction of Reading and Writing Difficulty: An Interactive Approach*, 3rd ed. Boston, MA: Allyn & Bacon.

Loera, G., Rueda, R., and Nakamoto, J. (2011). "The association between parental involvement in reading and schooling and children's reading engagement in Latino families." *Literacy Research and Instruction*, 50(2): 133–155.

Martin, E. J. and Hagan-Burke, S. (2002). "Establishing home-school connections: Strengthening the partnership between families and school." *Preventing School Failure*, 46(2): 62–65.

Moll, L., Amanti, C., Neff, S., and Gonzalez, N. (1992). Funds of knowledge for teaching: Using a qualitative approach to connect homes and school. *Theory into Practice*, 31(2): 132–141.

Successful Reading Assessments and Interventions

Paratore, J. R. (1995). "Implementing an intergenerational literacy project: Lessons learned." In L. M. Morrow (ed.), *Family Literacy Connections in Schools and Communities* (pp. 37–53). Newark, DE: International Reading Association, 37–53.

Shartrand, A. M., Weiss, H. B., Kreider, H. M., and Lopez, M. E. (1997). *New Skills for New Schools: Preparing Teachers in Family Involvement*. Retrieved January 6, 2011, from http://www.ed.gov/pubs/NewSkills/title.html.

Taylor, D. (1983). Family Literacy: Young children Learning to Read and Write. Portsmouth, NH: Heinemann.

Vang, C. (2006). "Minority parents should know more about school culture and its impact on their children's education." *Multicultural Education* 14(1): 20–26.

Villegas, A. M. and Lucas, T. (2002). "Preparing culturally responsive teachers: Rethinking the curriculum." *Journal of Teacher Education*, 53(1): 20–32.

Appendix 10-A   Parent Information*

Student's Name   Age   Grade   Birth Date

_____   _____   _____   _____

Person Being Interviewed   Relationship to Student

_____   _____

Can you tell me three positive things about your child?
1. _____

2. _____

3. _____

Environmental Information

Home Environment

Family Members Present in Home:

Name	Relationship to Student	Age	Birthplace	Occupation

Family Members Not Living in Home:

Name	Relationship to Student	Age	Birthplace	Occupation

Describe any reading or learning problems experienced by family members.

_____

_____

What reading activities, including reading to or with your child, are done at home? _____

_____

Describe your child's TV viewing. _____

_____

What are your child's responsibilities at home? _____

_____

What are the attitudes of family members toward reading? _____

_____

School Environment

Describe your child's preschool and kindergarten experiences. _____

_____

At what age did your child enter first grade? _____

_____

Describe your child's reading experiences in school so far. _____

_____

Has your child repeated any grade? If so, why? _____

_____

Describe your child's current school and classes, including any special placements or pullout programs. _____

_____

Describe the homework your child gets. _____

_____

How does your child do in areas other than reading, such as math, spelling, social studies, science, others _____

_____

Has your child's school attendance been regular? _____

_____

Describe any extended absences from school. _____

_____

Describe any testing your child has experienced in school. _____

_____

Describe any help your child has received outside of school. _____

_____

When did you first become concerned about your child's reading? _____

_____

Can you think of anything that might have contributed to your child's reading struggles? _____

_____

Social and Cultural Environment

Describe your child's relationship with other family members. _____

_____

What are your child's interests and leisure activities? _____

_____

Describe your child's friends. _____

_____

Physical Information

How would you compare your child's physical development with that of other children of the same age? _____

_____

Describe your child's general health _____

_____

Describe any illnesses, allergies, or accidents. _____

_____

Is your child taking any medication? _____

_____

Does your child seem to have difficulty paying attention? _____

_____

When was the last time your child's hearing was tested? _____

_____

When was the last time your child's vision was tested? _____

_____

Emotional Information

Does your child seem to be happy? _____

_____

Does your child exhibit any signs of emotional tension or lack of self-confidence?

_____

_____

What is your child's attitude toward reading? _____

_____

Language Development

What languages are spoken in the home? _____

_____

What languages does the child speak? _____

_____

How did your child's early language development compare with that of others?

_____

_____

Has your child received any bilingual or ELL services? _____

_____

Has your child received any speech or language therapy? _____

_____

Comments and Suggestions

Can you think of anything else we should know about in working with your
child? _____

_____

Does he or she have any special needs that we should take into consideration?

_____

_____

Appendix 10-B   Parent Interview

1. Tell me some of the favorite things your child likes to do. _____
   _____

2. Tell me some of the things your child does well. _____
   _____

3. What are your child's favorite television programs? _____
   _____

4. How much television does your child usually watch each day? On weekends? _____
   _____

5. Does your child play on a gaming system (xBox, PSP, etc.) _____
   _____

6. What games does your child like to play on the system? _____
   _____

7. Does your child participate in out-of-school activities? (e.g., sports, dance, art) _____
   _____

8. What chores does your child have at home? _____
   _____

9. How much homework is your child assigned each night? _____
   _____

10. Can your child complete the work on his/her own? _____
    _____

11. Tell me what kind of books your child seems to enjoy. _____
    _____

12. Tell me about your child's school experiences. _____
    _____

13. Tell me about your child's friends. _____
    _____

14. Why do you think your child was recommended to Literacy Space?
    _____
    _____

15. Is there anything else you would like to tell me? _____
    _____

Index